THE
HAUNTED
SOUTH

THE
HAUNTED
SOUTH

ALAN BROWN

Haunted America

Published by Haunted America
A Division of The History Press
Charleston, SC
www.historypress.com

Copyright © 2020 by Alan Brown
All rights reserved

First published 2020

Manufactured in the United States

ISBN 9781467148030

CONTENTS

CONTENTS

Contents

INTRODUCTION

The American South exists in many different incarnations. To the historian, the South is a place where a number of struggles took place, including the Revolutionary War, the Civil War and the civil rights movement. To romantics, the South is a fantasy world where beautiful ladies flitted around ballrooms and Southern colonels relaxed with mint juleps on the verandas of their Greek Revival plantation homes. To many African Americans, the South is a nightmarish world where their ancestors suffered under the lash and endured unspeakable atrocities. To many Native Americans, the South is the ancestral homeland from which they were forcibly removed. To people fascinated by the paranormal, the American South is a treasure-trove of ghost legends. The horrors of war and slavery have been preserved in stories that have been generated by battlefields, forts and plantations. Some of these uneasy spirits, people say, are still continuing their daily activities, oblivious to the fact that they are deceased. Others reappear in an effort to remind the living of the injustices that ended their lives. Still more spirits manifest themselves to reassure their friends and relatives that they are at peace in their new plane of existence.

Most of the stories in this book are legends. They are based in truth, but the facts have been distorted over the years through various retellings. Louisiana is heavily represented because it is generally regarded by paranormal investigators as the most haunted state in the South. This book contains a large number of stories from Alabama and Mississippi because I live and work in both of these states and am, therefore, very knowledgeable of their ghost stories. I have made an effort to feature tales that are not very well known outside of a particular region or state, although I did include updated stories about haunted places that are fairly famous, like the Myrtles in St. Francisville, Louisiana.

My purpose in this book is not to convince the reader that the paranormal is real or that the explanations I give for the occurrences in the stories are the only possible explanations. If you ask yourself when you finish reading, "Could this really have happened?" then I have accomplished my goal.

ALABAMA

BAY MINETTE

Bay Minette Public Library

The Women's Civic Improvement Association, under the leadership of Mrs. T.W. Gilmer (Anne) founded the Bay Minette Public Library in 1922. The public library was originally housed in one of the jury rooms of the courthouse. The library started out with four hundred books that had been given to it in a "book shower." Because the library did not have an operating budget, it ran on a subscription service provided by contributions from local merchants. The first librarian was Mrs. Anne Gilmer, who worked at the library from 1922 to 1943. In 1942, the library was moved to a rented room in the Stapleton building on Courthouse Square. In May 1930, the city council accepted a plan presented by Owen & Clark Architects in Mobile for a one-story colonial building. The new library, which opened its doors in December 1930, was named after Hampton D. Ewing, who donated the land for the city hall, police department and the public library. During the Great Depression, Mrs. Gilmer and her assistants did their best to keep the library in operation. With the help of the Works Progress Administration (WPA), the library was able to stay open every day. On October 4, 1943, Mrs. Gilmer was replaced by Mrs. Pearlie Overstreet. However, some members of the library staff believe that Mrs. Gilmer remained in the library long after her death.

In the book *Mobile Ghosts II: The Waterline*, library director Charlotte Jones Cabaniss Robertson told author Elizabeth Parker that she had heard that the library was haunted but did not put much stock in the tales until one day when she saw a book pushed all the way off one of the shelves and fall to the floor. After picking up and reshelving several books that had mysteriously "popped out," she began to notice a pattern: all of these books had been incorrectly shelved. Her suspicions that a ghostly librarian was trying to organize the library a little better were bolstered when a worker moved Mrs. Gilmer's portrait back to its original location over the main desk. Immediately, the worker smelled the scent of roses. Charlotte continued smelling roses when something good happened, such as an increase in the budget or a complimentary article in the local newspaper.

Eventually, the library outgrew its old location and moved across the street to the old Baptist church. Before she carried Mrs. Gilmer's portrait over to its new location, Charlotte invited her ghost to accompany her picture to its new home. The ghost seems to have taken Charlotte up on her offer. The first week the library was open, Charlotte was typing in her office late one evening when the elevator rose to the second floor. The door opened and closed, and the elevator went back down. The electrician who examined the elevator a couple of days later could find no rational explanation for the elevator's strange behavior. The possibility that the new library might also be haunted has never really bothered Charlotte very much because she always viewed Mrs. Gilmer's ghost as more of a guarding spirit than as a malevolent, terrifying presence.

BIRMINGHAM

Arlington

Arlington is one of the few antebellum homes in the Birmingham area. According to many sources, Arlington was built by William Mudd in 1842. However, a former director of Arlington, Mrs. Catherine M. Lackmon, believes that the first wing of the house was built about twenty years later by Stephen Hall, who purchased 475 acres on April 21, 1821, near the town of Elyton. Hall's will mentions a "dwelling house and outhouses thereunto belong," which were probably constructed in 1822. The house stood on a wooded knoll just off the old Georgia Road. Hall, a cotton planter, became one of the wealthiest men in the county.

By 1842, Hall had accumulated so much debt that the land was sold at public auction in front of the courthouse of Jefferson County in Elyton to attorney William S. Mudd for $700. Four years later, he bought a neighboring tract of eighty acres. Instead of tearing down the existing house and starting over, Mudd added the east wing, copying the architectural style of the west wing. Mudd's intention was to create a colonnaded mansion for his new bride. Mudd, who eventually became a judge, enjoyed receiving guests at his lavish new home. Before Long, Mudd's home became the social hub of Elyton's social set.

On March 28, 1865, Mudd was forced to play the role of reluctant host when Wilson's Raiders, 13,500 strong, entered Jefferson County. During his two-hour stay in what he described as a "poor, insignificant Southern village," Union general James Harrison Wilson commandeered Mudd's home for his headquarters. The general and his staff resided on the first floor, while Mudd, his wife and his four daughters stayed upstairs. From Arlington's luxurious sitting room, Wilson ordered his Raiders to destroy munitions, factories and the University of Alabama.

Mudd was entertaining the poet Mary Gordon Duffee when Wilson's troops made their unexpected arrival. Duffee was leading a double life as a newspaper reporter and as a Confederate spy. To keep her safe from the Yankee intruders, Mudd hid her in the attic. When she overheard the general's plans to destroy the iron furnaces at Tannehill, Duffee snuck out of the attic in the dead of night so that she could warn the workers of the impending invasion. Ironically, the unwelcome visit by Wilson's Raiders probably saved the mansion from destruction. After the Civil War, Colonel James Powell, Josiah Morris and John Milner sipped brandy and smoked cigars at Mudd's home while planning the creation of a new town just east of Elyton to be called Birmingham.

After the Civil War, descendants of the Mudd family moved to Birmingham. The size of the estate dwindled over the years. Following Mudd's death in 1884, ownership of the house changed hands several times. The Mudd family sold the house to Henry Bardleben, a Birmingham entrepreneur, who sold off all but thirty-three acres before finally deeding the land over to Franklin H. Whitney of Iowa. Whitney divided the property into lots and rechristened it "Arlington Survey" in honor of his idol, General Robert E. Lee. Under Whitney's ownership, Arlington was inhabited around the turn of the century by a German immigrant family and by a black newspaper editor and his wife, who lived in a frame house in the front yard.

After Whitney died in 1896, Arlington passed into the hands of Robert Sylvester Munger in 1902. Munger was a Texas philanthropist who had amassed a fortune for inventing a method of removing harmful lint thrown off during the cleaning of cotton seed in the ginning process. By the time Munger had become the new owner, Arlington was in serious need of repair. He not only renovated the house but also added such modern conveniences as indoor plumbing, central heat and electricity. Arlington served as the Munger family's summer retreat until 1910, when they made the home their permanent residence. After Munger's death in 1914, one of his daughters, Mrs. Alex G. Montgomery, inherited the property.

When Ruby and Alex Montgomery bought the house and property in 1924, the estate had been reduced to only six acres. In 1951, the Montgomerys decided that Arlington was not a suitable residence for only two people, and they decided to convert the property into a subdivision. Convinced that Arlington should be transformed into a shrine instead, a group called the Birmingham Historic Committee initiated a campaign to raise funds to save the old mansion. Individuals, business firms and almost every civic group in Birmingham donated money to the campaign. By 1953, the Birmingham Historic Committee had raised $25,000 toward the $50,000 purchase price. The City of Birmingham added another $25,000 and agreed to underwrite the mansion's operation costs, which would be offset in part by an admission charge once guided tours were offered in the home.

Since Arlington was first opened to the public in 1953, the Arlington Historical Association has tried to restore the mansion to the way it would have looked between 1842 and 1875. A number of individuals have donated period furnishings, such as an Empire sofa and an ebony square grand piano, circa 1840; two Enfield rifles, 1862–63; a mahogany Hepplewhite banquet table inlaid with light-colored satinwood, 1780; and a Sheraton sideboard with serpentine front, 1810.

In 1985, the Arlington Historical Association raised $70,000 to renovate the old mansion. Chips of paint were analyzed to determine the home's original color, which turned out to be a creamy white. Layers of bricks on Arlington's four chimneys were stabilized with the help of the city's traffic-engineering department. Shutter workers patented by Frank B. Mallory of Orange, New Jersey, in 1886 were cleaned and repaired. Workers also re-plastered the walls and replaced sections of the wooden handrail on the central staircase that had rotted. The outdoor kitchen was transformed into the gift shop.

Like many antebellum homes in the South, Arlington has a storied past. Elderly residents of Birmingham still talk about seeing a Civil War saber sticking out of an ancient oak that stood in front of Arlington, the city's only remaining antebellum mansion. According to the legend, a young woman who lived at Arlington fell in love with a young man from a neighboring plantation. They were engaged to be married, but like so many young couples in 1861, they decided to postpone their wedding until the war ended. Just before leaving with his regiment, the young man was saying goodbye to his sweetheart beneath the shade of a young oak tree. Desperate to prove his undying love, he thrust his sword through the tree trunk and vowed to remove it upon his safe return. Like so many young soldiers eager to prove themselves in battle, the young man died, and his fiancée refused to allow the sword to be removed from the tree. Over the years, the tree grew around the sword, leaving only its hilt and tip visible. One could still see the sword protruding from the tree well into the twentieth century.

This romantic story bears a strong resemblance to similar Civil War legends collected throughout the South. However, Birmingham's version of the story is much more than just a fanciful tale. In fact, the true story of the sword in the tree is almost as unbelievable as the legend itself.

Although I had heard the legend of the sword in the tree for many years, my interest in the legend was revived in June 2002. While speaking to a group of senior citizens at St. Martin's in the Pines, I learned that the story is true and that the sword is on display in the parlor. In July, I visited Arlington and was surprised to find that the "sword" mounted to the wall of the parlor was not a sword at all but the blade of a scythe. Food services supervisor Stephen R. Moode gave me the true account of Arlington's most enduring legend:

> *This is the version I have heard. As you can tell, it's not really a sword. It's a scythe. At the time of the Civil War, there was another plantation over by Legion Field. One of the soldiers in Elyton who was going to war pledged his love to the girl who lived there. He told her he'd love her forever. Just before his company marched off to war, he picked up a scythe and shoved it through a little oak tree. He told the girl, "As long as this sword stays in the tree, I will love you." Of course, he got killed in the war, and she never pulled the scythe out.*

Steve went on to say that over time, the handle of the scythe eventually rotted off, leaving only the rusted blade in the tree. In the 1960s, during the construction of an apartment, the old oak tree was cut down, and the chunk of wood containing the scythe blade was taken to Arlington. After the wood rotted away, the scythe disappeared. "We couldn't find it anywhere," Steve said. "Then four years ago, when we were remodeling the house, I was on a ladder in the front parlor. I was up on the ladder, and I looked down—and guess where the scythe was. It was on top of the secretary. It has a very deep crown, and nobody could ever see it. I brought the scythe into the dining room where we were having our Thursday luncheon. I went up to our director and said, 'Dan, I hate to bother you, but I've got something to show you. Is this what you've been looking for?' He said, 'Oh, my! Let me see it.' He added that the staff members at Arlington had been looking for that thing for many years. The scythe had probably been put there back in the late 1970s or the early 1980s. No one really knows why."

Apparently, the fate of the "sword" in the tree is not the only mystery that has been generated at the antebellum home. In recent years, guests and staff members have reported a number of seemingly paranormal incidents in the home. Guests have seen rocking chairs move by themselves, as if someone were sitting in them. Docents have heard doors slamming in the house on days when no one else was present. Some people have also felt as if they are being watched by "unseen" eyes. The identity of the ghost has never been determined, probably because so many different families have lived in the house over the years. However, a likely candidate would be the spirit of the girl whose lover was killed in the Civil War before he could remove the scythe from the tree.

The story of the sword in the tree, along with the mystery of its disappearance, is a good example of a traveling legend. In the version still circulating in Birmingham, Arlington is the setting of the lovers' farewell, and the rather utilitarian scythe has been replaced by the much more glamorous sword. Convincing the citizens of Birmingham that the "old" version of the story is false would probably be just as difficult as filling in all the blanks in the historical account.

GULF SHORES

Fort Morgan

The first fort built on Mobile Point was erected by the Americans in 1813 during the War of 1812. This mud-and-earth redoubt was named Fort Boyer. The rude fort sustained an attack by the British navy and army in 1814 during the First Battle of Fort Boyer. However, the fort surrendered to the British in the Second Battle of Fort Boyer in 1815, a few months after the signing of the Treaty of Ghent on Christmas Eve in 1814. Convinced that brick-and-mortar forts were the country's best defense against a land and sea attack, the United States began building a series of forts along the Gulf Coast.

The construction of one of these forts, Fort Morgan, began in 1818 with the hiring of a contractor named Benjamin Hopkins. Hopkins died a year later of yellow fever and was replaced by Samuel Hawkins, but Hawkins died of the fever in 1821. Captain R.E. DeRussey was then assigned the task of building the fort with slave labor. After DeRussey became sick in 1825,

Fort Morgan, Gulf Shores, Alabama. *Courtesy of the Library of Congress.*

the fort was completed by his deputy, Lieutenant Cornelius Ogden, in 1834. Before the construction of the fort was completed, two of the contractors had gone bankrupt due to the delays caused by the inaccessibility of the site. It was named after General Daniel Morgan, a hero of the American Revolution. Over forty million bricks went into the construction of the fort. Each of the fort's five faces has seven arched brick casemates. Between 1834 and 1837, Fort Morgan was an important stop along the Trail of Tears. Beginning in 1842, Fort Morgan was deactivated and was not garrisoned again for nineteen years.

Ironically, Fort Morgan was taken by a small force of four companies of Alabama volunteers on January 3, 1861, just eight days before Alabama seceded from the Union. Eighteen of the fort's heaviest guns were placed facing the channel to provide protective fire for blockade runners. Colonel Charles Stewart served as commander of Fort Morgan from October 1862 until April 30, 1863. Stewart was killed instantly during the test firing of a cannon that exploded.

For the first three years of the war, Fort Morgan did not face any serious threat from Federal forces. The first true test of Fort Morgan came on August 5, 1864, when the Union fleet, under the command of Admiral David Farragut, launched a devastating attack against the fort. After one of the fleet's four ironclads, the USS *Tecumseh*, was blown up by a mine or torpedo, Admiral Farragut spurred his sailors with the words, "Damn the torpedoes. Full speed ahead!"

Almost instantly, Farragut's fleet surged ahead toward the bay. As the Federal gunships positioned themselves a safe distance from Fort Morgan's cannons, the Confederate ironclad CSS *Tennessee* was engaged in running battles with as many as seven Union ships at the same time. By the time the CSS *Tennessee* finally sank, it had engaged thirteen ships in battle.

After Fort Gaines surrendered, Federal troops initiated a land assault against the fort. During the siege, a ten-sided barracks inside the fort was set afire. Fort Morgan withstood a steady bombardment of more than three thousand shells from the Federal warships for two weeks. During the shelling, cannons were knocked off their mounts, and bricks were shattered. Before General Richard L. Page finally surrendered on August 23, 1864, the defenders had destroyed thousands of pounds of gunpowder and spiked the cannon. For the remainder of the Civil War, Fort Morgan remained in the hands of the Union, which used it as a base for reconnaissance raids and as a staging area for the Battle of Fort Blakely.

A couple walking along the top of Fort Morgan was followed by the ghost of a Confederate soldier. *Courtesy of the author.*

Fort Morgan was renovated several times after the Civil War. After twelve two-hundred-pounder Parrott rifled cannons were installed in the fort in the 1870s, the U.S. government abandoned the fort. Then between 1895 and 1900, five concrete batteries were constructed in the fort. Hurricanes heavily damaged the wooden buildings along Officers Row in 1906 and 1916. In 1915, an experimental battery, Battery Test, was built in the fort by the Coast Artillery Corps. After it became clear that Battery Test could withstand cannon fire from two battleships, the gun was moved to a different location. Between 1917 and 1919, coast artillerymen were trained in the use of modern weapons at Fort Morgan. Four British 9.2-inch howitzers were moved to the fort in 1920, but they were scrapped in 1924 after Fort Morgan was abandoned once again. The old fort was reactivated in April 1942, when the military reoccupied the complex.

During World War II, the concrete batteries were no longer the fort's primary defensive positions. Five World War I–vintage guns were mounted on top of Fort Morgan. In 1946, Fort Morgan was turned over to the State of Alabama. In 1960, it was declared a National Historic Landmark.

Visitors have had strange encounters inside Fort Morgan ever since it was first opened to the general public. A number of people have seen full-bodied apparitions just outside the old fort. Two young men who were walking around the fort late at night spotted a lone male figure standing near the tree line. He appeared to be staring out at the bay. By the time the young men had rounded the point and returned to the tree line, the apparition was gone. Around the same time, two boys were fishing near Fort Morgan very early in the morning when they saw a strange-looking man standing on the beach, staring out at the ocean. Even though the boys were talking and laughing, the man totally ignored them. Within a few minutes, the apparition slowly faded away. A number of people have also seen a pair of Civil War soldiers walking down Fort Morgan Road at midnight. In the late 2000s, a woman and her husband were fishing on the beach just behind Fort Morgan. While her husband stood in the water, casting his line, she sat in the sand, watching him. Suddenly, she felt as if she was being watched. She turned around and noticed a woman in a Victorian-era dress standing behind her. She realized she was in the presence of the paranormal when the woman disappeared.

People walking inside the fort have also had strange experiences. Many tourists have reported hearing blood-curdling screams and the rattling of chains inside Fort Morgan. Some visitors have felt as if someone was standing beside them in the darkened rooms. Others claim to have been touched inside the arched rooms. Many visitors have heard footsteps walking right to them and stopping in front of them. They then hear someone speaking so closely in their ears that they can feel the entity's breath. One guest said that he was walking through one of the rooms when something threw him to the ground. In the late 1990s, a little boy and his parents who were touring the fort decided to take a group picture inside one of the rooms before leaving. When they returned to the car, the boy was looking over the pictures they had taken when he noticed the image of a transparent male figure passing through one of the walls. On another occasion, a man and his wife were walking on top of the fort when they turned around and noticed a man in a tattered Confederate uniform walking behind them. When they waved at the man, whom they assumed was a reenactor, he jumped off the wall. The couple immediately ran down the steps to the spot where the soldier would have landed but were unable to find any evidence that someone had just jumped onto the mounds of sand just outside the fort.

In 2008, a group of ghost hunters called Bon Secour Paranormal Investigations spent the night at Fort Morgan in an effort to determine the validity of the stories they had been hearing. The group members collected a number of eerie electronic voice phenomena (EVPs) during their

Above: Apparitions of soldiers have been seen standing and walking outside the fort. *Courtesy of the author.*

Right: Visitors walking through the casements have heard voices and the sound of footsteps walking behind them. *Courtesy of the author.*

investigation, including "Help us," "It ain't worth it," "Here we go" and "You're all in." One of their cameras captured a mist-like form that was moving through the fort. A number of orbs showed up in their photographs, including one that seemed to have two eyes, a nose and a mouth.

Fort Morgan has changed a great deal since the Civil War. None of the fort's original wooden structures remain. The lighthouse keeper's house, built in 1872, is the oldest wooden building on the site. All five of the other wooden structures, such as the Administration Building (1898) and the senior officers' buildings, were built in the late 1800s and the early 1900s. These buildings are all that is left of the almost one hundred structures that once made up the complex. However, one aspect of Fort Morgan's past that shows no signs of disappearing very soon is its ghost stories.

MAUVILLA

Kali Oka Road

Kali Oka Road is a narrow, two-lane gravel road off Highway 45 North, just past Kushla and Mauvilla. This old road is one of those out-of-the-way spots frequently visited by high school and college students looking for supernatural thrills. After carefully making their way around the colorfully named "Dead Man's Curve," young people drive down to Cry Baby Bridge.

Cry Baby Bridge is the second of the two bridges just past Oak Grove Road on Kali Oka Road. According to one of the legends, a woman standing on the bridge late one night in the 1950s threw her newborn infant over the side to spite her husband. A totally different legend has it that a woman driving down Kali Oka Road late one night plunged over the side of the bridge, killing herself and her baby. In still another tale, a little boy drowned after being accidentally pushed off the bridge by his friends.

In recent years, people have claimed that their engines stalled just as they were driving over the bridge. Young people standing on the bridge have heard a loud splashing sound, followed by unearthly cries. A few people have discovered tiny handprints on their windows after driving over the bridge. One young man said that he found a small child's muddy footprints on his car after returning home. Ghost hunters have captured orbs on and around the bridge with their digital cameras. At least two young men claim to have been tossed off the bridge by an invisible force.

A number of attempts have been made to debunk the ghosts of Kali Oka Road over the years. Some say that the screams people have heard while standing on Cry Baby Bridge are the cries of one of the rare black panthers that are said to roam the woods in South Alabama. However, witnesses who have had their hair stand on end or felt goosebumps rise on their skin on dark, gloomy nights have proven to be difficult to convince. Please respect the privacy of people living on Kali Oka Road and Oak Grove Road.

MOBILE

The USS *Alabama*

When the keel for the USS *Alabama* was laid at the Norfolk Navy Yard on February 1, 1940, it was the sixth ship to bear the name Alabama, the most famous being the CSS *Alabama*, under the command of Captain Raphael Semmes. Coincidentally, Semmes's great-grandson served in the U.S. Navy and was stationed on the USS *Alabama* during World War II. Construction of the BB-60—the USS *Alabama*'s official designation—was completed almost two years later, and it was christened on August 16, 1942, by the wife of Alabama senator Lister Hill. On November 11, 1942, the USS *Alabama* began a series of training exercises in the Chesapeake Bay area under the command of Captain George B. Wilson. Captain Fred D. Kirtland relieved Captain Wilson as skipper of the USS *Alabama* on March 20, 1943.

After protecting lend-lease convoys to Britain and Russia, the USS *Alabama* reported for duty in the Pacific with the Third Fleet at New Hebrides in September 1943. The crew of the USS *Alabama* first saw action on February 12, 1944, when the battleship's massive guns bombarded Truk Island. It was also part of the force that raided the Palau Islands. Between April 29 and May 1, 1944, the USS *Alabama* pounded Ponape and Truk, not long after General Douglas MacArthur's troops had landed at Hollandia, Ataipe and Humboldt Bay in New Guinea. The battleship's next engagement was at the Battle of the Philippine Sea, where it and other members of the fleet shot down nine Japanese planes. The USS *Alabama* steamed over to Guam for pre-invasion and D-Day support on July 6, 1944.

The USS *Alabama* was decommissioned on January 9, 1945. It was towed to Mobile Bay in 1964. *Courtesy of the author.*

After Captain Vincent R. Murphy relieved Captain Kirtland as skipper, the USS *Alabama* assisted with the capture of the Southern Carolines and the Palaus in September 1944. The USS *Alabama* and other ships fended off attack from Japanese fighters during the Leyte operation and then moved south, eventually joining Admiral "Bull" Halsey's fleet in an attack off Cape Ehgano as part of the Battle of Leyte Gulf on October 25, 1944. The USS *Alabama* had just ridden out a typhoon during the Mindaro operation when it was notified on December 24, 1944, that it was to be overhauled on the West Coast of the United States. In May 1945, the USS *Alabama* returned to Ulithi and participated in the Third and Fifth Fleets' raids on the Japanese home island in the Okinawa Gunto. On May 4, 1945, the USS *Alabama* was in the middle of an attack by five kamikaze planes. One of the kamikazes crashed into the flagship, the USS *Enterprise*. The USS *Alabama* shot down two of the four remaining planes.

The USS *Alabama* was slightly damaged in another typhoon on June 5, 1945. Five days later, the battleship bombarded Minami Daito Jima. The USS *Alabama* lay at anchor for three weeks before rejoining the Third Fleet and participating in an assault on the home islands of Japan. On July 17, 1945, the USS *Alabama* lobbed shell after shell on the engineering works on Honshu Island, only fifty miles north of Tokyo, during a heavy thunderstorm.

Following the surrender of Japan on September 2, 1945, the USS *Alabama* dropped anchor at Tokyo Bay. It transported 3,700 passengers from Okinawa to the United States. The USS *Alabama* and other members of the Third Fleet celebrated Navy Day in San Francisco on October 27, 1945. The "Mighty A" made its final voyage to Bremerton, Washington, where it was decommissioned on January 9, 1945.

In 1964, the people of Mobile launched a campaign to fund the towing of the USS *Alabama* to Mobile Bay. With the assistance of the $100,000 raised by Alabama schoolchildren and over $900,000 of corporate support, the USS *Alabama* made its way to its final resting place at USS *Alabama* Battleship Memorial Park. Judging from tales told by visitors to the fine old battleship, the USS *Alabama* might have brought along with it the spirits of some of the valiant men who died in service.

The first tragedies were two workers who died during the construction of the USS *Alabama* at Norfolk, Virginia. Although no sailors died as the result of enemy fire during the battleship's three years of service during World War II, eight men perished as the result of friendly fire when gun

Eight sailors died when gun mount number 9 accidentally fired on gun mount number 5. *Courtesy of the author.*

A spectral hand pulled an earring from a woman's ear in the sleeping quarters. *Courtesy of the author.*

mount number 9 fired on gun mount number 5. The interior of the turret was plastered with the bloody remains of the gun crew. Nothing remained of the gun commander but his boots. After these deaths, the workers sleeping in the marine compartment heard disembodied footsteps walking around the corner in their direction. No one else was on board the battleship at the time.

Ghostly footsteps have been reported throughout the battleship. The ghost of a blond sailor was sighted in the officers' quarters. A spectral cook has been seen preparing meals in the mess hall. Late at night, people have heard the steel watertight hatch doors slam shut by themselves. Strange tapping and popping sounds have been heard in the bulkheads, and tourists have felt an overwhelming sense of melancholy while walking through the ship. One visitor claimed that a disembodied hand snatched her earring from her ear in the sleeping quarters.

The staff at the USS *Alabama* Battleship Park has dismissed rumors that the old battleship is haunted. Park officials offer as proof the fact that none of the 160,000 people who have spent the night on the USS *Alabama* have reported any paranormal activity. If any convincing photographs or orbs are ever collected, the USS *Alabama* will join the ranks of other haunted battleships from the World War II era, such as the USS *Hornet* and the USS *North Carolina.*

Seaman's Bethel Theatre
(University of South Alabama)

The University of South Alabama (USA) was founded in May 1963. It was the first university in the state to be chartered since the University of Montevallo was founded in 1893, and it was also a desegregated university.

After USA's first president, Fred Widdon, successfully petitioned the state legislature for more funding in March 1965, the university began purchasing several historic structures. The Tuthill Townhouse (1845) was acquired in 1965. In 1968, USA bought the Seamen's Bethel Chapel and the Toulmin House. Two years later, the old Saenger Theater in downtown Mobile was converted into a university theater. In the 1980s, the University of South Alabama bought the old Providence Hospital for the purpose of housing the College of Nursing. In the late 1980s and early 1990s, USA added other old buildings to the campus, such as Doctors Hospital and Knollwood Park Hospital. Not surprisingly, one of these historic structures introduced some old spirits to the relatively new campus.

Built in 1860, the Seaman's Bethel was originally located in downtown Mobile, where it served as a refuge for indigent sailors. Over a century later, it was moved to the campus of the University of South Alabama, where it served for many years as a theater-in-the-round for the Drama Department. For over a decade, the former chapel housed the USA Honors Program. The older members used the building's ghost stories to "break the ice" when new members were inducted.

One of the stories they told was about the basement. Actors who were getting dressed in the costume shop reported catching glimpses of a small child running around the racks of hanging clothes. People have also heard the high-pitched giggles of a youngster in the basement hallways. Another haunted part of the Seaman's Bethel Theatre was the fly loft, where stage crews, actors and members of the audience have seen the tall figure of a sailor. Witnesses describe the striking male figure as wearing a sailor's cap and a captain's coat.

In the fall of 2011, the Honors Program was scheduled to move from the Seaman's Bethel Theatre to Faculty Court West after the Colleges of Computer Information Systems and Engineering moved into Shelby Hall. At the same time, the basement was remodeled to house the fundraising headquarters of the Office of Development and Alumni Relations. The ground floor was renovated as well. Experts in the paranormal believe that the paranormal activity could resume after the structural changes are made, or the ghosts could leave altogether as they search for a new theater.

Fort Gaines

Up until the nineteenth century, Dauphin Island had been home to a small French colony that was set up in the early 1700s. At the time, the island was known as "Massacre Island" because French explorer Pierre Le Moyne had found a huge pile of Indian bones when he arrived there in 1699. The island was renamed Dauphin Island in honor of the heir to the French throne, the Dauphin. In 1711, Dauphin Island was devastated by a pirate attack, and in 1717, the colony was almost completely destroyed by a massive hurricane.

The United States showed no real interest in Dauphin Island until the War of 1812, when the need for more coastal defenses became readily apparent. The construction of the new fort on Mobile Bay began in 1821, but progress was impeded by high tides and mounting costs. Congress appropriated $20,000 for the project in 1845, but construction stalled once again, this time because of land disputes. Eight years later, the federal government gained clear title to the building site. Chief Engineer Joseph G. Totten decided to jettison the original building plan and create a fort that would be a city unto itself. Totten wanted to mount guns on each of the fort's five walls. Four howitzers would be placed in each bastion. The fort's twenty-two-foot-high brick-and-sand walls, which were four and a half feet thick at the top, would absorb the concussion of a bombardment. Work crews dug a moat thirty-five feet away from the base of the fort to make it less vulnerable from the land side. Totten believed that his vision for the new fort would insulate it from attack by land and sea.

In 1853, Congress named the fort after General Edmund Pendleton Gaines, who had led the detachment that captured Aaron Burr and the defense of Fort Erie during the War of 1812. Construction of Fort Gaines was almost completed in 1861 before the attack on Fort Sumter. Confederate engineers added the finishing touches. Fort Gaines was the center of operations for blockade runners, who brought goods in and out of Mobile Bay. The Battle of Mobile Bay was waged between August 2 and August 23, 1864, to shut down the city's blockade-running efforts. The mighty cannons mounted on the fort's walls inflicted considerable damage onto the Union fleet, under the command of Admiral David G. Farragut.

Fort Gaines became strategically important after the Civil War as well. In 1898, three six-inch disappearing naval guns and three rapid-fire three-inch guns were mounted around the walls, eliminating the need for corner bastions. Concrete gun mounts were constructed on the easterly walls. During

Fort Gaines. *Courtesy of the Library of Congress.*

World War I, a coastal artillery unit garrison manned the fort's disappearing guns. During this time, Fort Gaines, also served as an antiaircraft gunnery school. The old Civil War fort was used as a base for the U.S. Coast Guard and as a camp for the Alabama National Guard between 1941 and 1945. The coast guard still conducts rescue boat operations from its base at Fort Gaines. The fort was sold to the City of Mobile in 1926. Fort Gaines is now operated by the Dauphin Island Park and Beach Board.

Fort Gaines is reputed to be haunted, either by the men who served there or by the Union sailors who died while attacking the fort in 1864. The ghosts of Union and Confederate soldiers have been sighted wandering through the fort. Some visitors claim that a spectral soldier they encountered inside the fort followed them to the front gate and then abruptly disappeared. Ghostly figures dressed in tattered uniforms have been seen standing inside the bastions and perched on top of the bunkers outside the walls. Staff members and visitors alike have heard phantom footsteps throughout the fort. A resident of Dauphin Island was driving to the turnaround behind Fort Gaines with an old fraternity brother when both men saw a woman in a long, white dress staring out at the ocean. She then turned around and gazed for a few seconds at the two men in the car before fading away.

A number of paranormal investigations have been conducted at Fort Gaines. In the early 2000s, crew members of the MTV television show *Fear* visited the old fort. They claimed to have detected the presence of a

Native American woman wearing animal furs standing inside the fort. The investigators said that she was covered with blood at the time. The film crew concluded that some of the Native American ghosts that have been seen within the fort are the spirits of men and women who were killed in one of the tunnels during a cave-in during the late nineteenth century. Another fatal event at the fort involves several soldiers who were trying to escape through an underground pipe. They drowned when the water from high tides washed over them. Bones have been known to wash out of the hillside occasionally, providing credibility to these legends of mass death. These burials in unsanctified ground could explain why Fort Gaines is filled with so many restless spirits.

Central Fire Station

Mobile's Central Fire Station was built in 1925 at 701 St. Francis Street. It was dedicated to Laz Schwartz, who had served as mayor and commissioner from 1911 to 1917 before passing away in 1925. The new fire station was equipped with a state-of-the-art alarm system, the Gamewell Alarm System. At the time, telephones were not widely available to the general public, so "pull boxes" were installed on street corners. Pulling a lever on the box sent a signal to the fire department, notifying firefighters of the location of the box. The old alarm system was deactivated in the 1960s. In 2009, the alarm room was converted into the Fire Station Museum.

On August 16, 2010, something happened in the Fire Station Museum that catapulted the Central Fire Station into the spotlight. Early in the morning, light number four (a blue light) and light number ten (a red light) turned on by themselves. The firefighters were understandably perplexed because the power to the panel had been torn out years before.

Many firemen believe that the entity responsible for the weird events of April 16 is the ghost of Mayor Laz Schwartz, whose presence in the old fire station has been felt for a long time. Firemen have reported seeing the shadowy figure of a man walking through the building. Objects that were placed in a specific room the night before have been found in an entirely different location the next morning.

A rational explanation has been suggested for the lighting up of the old alarm system. The station's computers had been thrown offline by lightning just two days before. Did residual electricity light up the tubes, or is residual spirit activity responsible for resurrecting the Gamewell Alarm System?

The Bragg-Mitchell Mansion

The Bragg-Mitchell Mansion was built in 1855 by John Bragg, who studied law at the University of North Carolina–Chapel Hill. After passing the bar exam in 1824, Hill set up a law practice in Mobile. He was appointed judge to Alabama's Tenth Judicial Court in 1842. After his election to the Thirty-second United States Congress, Hill resigned his position as judge. He purchased the property at 1906 Springhill Avenue, where he built his dream house for $7,500. He constructed the mansion so that he and his family had a place to live during Mobile's social season, which lasted from Thanksgiving through Mardi Gras. The rest of the year, the Braggs lived at their plantation in Lowndes County.

Like most property owners in Mobile, Judge Hill's comfortable life was interrupted by the advent of the Civil War. The story goes that he removed all of the live oak trees on his land to make it easier for the Confederate army to spot the advancing Union troops. Just before the arrival of Wilson's Raiders, John Bragg moved all of the mansion's luxurious furniture, carpeting, mirrors and paintings to his plantation in Lowndes County. After the Civil War, John's brother, Confederate general Braxton Bragg, was a frequent guest at the mansion.

The Bragg-Mitchell House. *Courtesy of the Library of Congress.*

Two years after John Bragg's death on August 10, 1878, the mansion was sold to William H. Pratt. Bragg's former home passed through a series of owners, including the Upham, Davis and Wingate families before it was purchased by A.S. Mitchell in 1931 for $20,000. The Mitchell family lived in the mansion until 1965. The A.S. Mitchell foundation donated the Bragg-Mitchell Mansion to the Explore Center in the late 1970s with the intention of converting it into an interactive science museum. To preserve the historical authenticity of the old house, the decision was made to build a separate science museum, the Gulf Coast Exploreum.

Following the mansion's placement on the National Register of Historic Places, it was extensively renovated at the cost of $3 million. The Bragg-Mitchell Mansion was opened to the general public and now hosts such local events as corporate dinners and wedding receptions. Today, the old mansion is not only one of the most photographed buildings in Mobile but one of the most haunted as well.

In her book *Mobile Ghosts: Alabama's Haunted Port City*, author Elizabeth Parker says that the ghosts of the Bragg-Mitchell Mansion have manifested themselves in a number of different ways. Disembodied voices have been heard throughout the old mansion. A woman who was upstairs heard a ghostly sneeze so real that the woman said, "God bless you!" The massive front door has opened and closed on its own. Sometimes the elevator moves up and down between the floors by itself. A repairman who was working on the air conditioning in the attic was unable to get out after someone—or something—locked the attic door. After a wedding was held inside the mansion, a large flower vase that had been placed on a table before the mansion was closed was found on its side underneath the table the next morning.

Restoring the Bragg-Mitchell Mansion's nineteenth-century elegance has been an ongoing process ever since the home was first opened to the public. In fact, one of the old home's primary missions is to give visitors the feeling that they have stepped back into the antebellum era as they stroll through the buildings and grounds. The mansion's resident ghosts seem to be doing their part to bring the past into the twenty-first century.

The Richards-DAR House

The beautiful brick Italianate house at 256 Joachim Street was built for a riverboat captain from Maine, Charles G. Richards; his bride, Caroline

Richards-DAR House, Mobile, Alabama. *Courtesy of the Library of Congress.*

Richards; and their eight surviving children in 1860. Sadly, Caroline died in childbirth in 1862.

Like many of Mobile's antebellum homes, the Richards home survived the Civil War totally unscathed. For a short period in the twentieth century, the Richards home was operated as a bed-and-breakfast. Members of the Richards family lived in the family home until 1946, when it was sold to the Ideal Cement Company. The first floor of the old house was used as offices, and the second floor was reserved for guests and company officials who wished to spend the night in Mobile. The company also restored the carriage house and added brick pavers to the driveway.

The City of Mobile acquired the home in 1973. The house is now the headquarters of the Daughters of the American Revolution (DAR). Members of Mobile's six DAR chapters serve as docents and caretakers.

The house is distinguished by a number of striking architectural features, including Carrara marble fireplaces, ruby glass panes at the front entrance, the immense crystal chandelier in the dining room, its ornate French mirror and its beautifully etched glass globes. Only two of the 1870s-era furnishings belonged to the Richards family: a portrait of Caroline Richards's brother and a square grand piano. The Richards-DAR House is best known for the wrought-iron fence on the front façade. The paranormal activity that has been reported inside the house over the years is probably its best-kept secret.

According to the docents, most of ghostly activity in the Richards-DAR House takes the form of strange noises, usually when the docents are getting the house ready for guests early in the morning. Many people have heard the sound of children playing in the Richards-DAR House, especially on the circular staircase and in the second-floor hallway. In an interview with Elizabeth Parker, author of *Mobile Ghosts: Alabama's Haunted Port City*, DAR member Ann Biggs said childish laughter emanates from the closed-in porch as well. "They kept the boys out there to play, though they kept the girls inside, close to father," Biggs said. "You'll hear them running up there, playing chase." Ann Biggs and one of the former tour guides have also seen the figure of a woman, presumably the ghost of Caroline Richards, staring out the window in the red bedroom, as if she is checking out the grounds. The docents have also heard the loud, stern voice of a woman inside the house. They believe that the spectral voice belongs to the spirit of Caroline Richards, who is scolding her children for misbehaving.

The Richards-DAR House is similar to hundreds of other museum homes in that its primary source of income is the revenue generated by receptions, meetings and weddings. Flag Day ceremonies at the old home are also a major attraction. Docents dressed in period costumes give tours and offer visitors a cup of spice tea served with cookies. Apparently, the old home's resident spirits do their part to entertain guests as well.

Oakleigh Plantation

James Mason was a dry goods merchant, cotton commission merchant and brick mason from James City County, Virginia. Soon after he arrived in Mobile, he established a brickyard on Walter Street in downtown Mobile, where the Battle House Tower now stands. The site that he selected for his T-shaped Greek Revival mansion was thirty-five acres of woodland just west of Mobile. This location was ideal because of a nearby clay pit, from which bricks for his house could be made. He also used timber from the forests on his property in the construction of his house. Surrounded by majestic oak trees, his home, named Oakleigh, boasted several innovations. The windows were designed to circulate air through the house on sultry summer days. Oakleigh's most interesting feature was its second-story gallery, which was reached by a curved staircase from the terrace below.

Mason's life-long dream of building a Greek temple on top of a small hill was finally realized in 1833, when his house was completed, but his elation was dampened by the death of his wife and child a short time before. His fortunes continued to decline during the Panic of 1837, when the bank repossessed his house because of his inability to pay back the $20,000 he had borrowed to build it. Fortunately for Roper, his brother-in-law, Boyd Simison, purchased Oakleigh and allowed Roper to live there rent-free with his second wife and six children.

In 1850, Roper moved to New Orleans; the next year, the house was rented to Alfred Irwin, treasurer of the Mobile & Ohio Railroad. Irwin purchased the house in 1852. Legend has it that Irwin's wife, Margaret, a British citizen, prevented the Yankees from burning Oakleigh by declaring her property neutral territory and hanging the Union Jack from the balcony. In the years preceding and immediately following the Civil War, Alfred and Margaret Irwin entertained some of Mobile's most prominent citizens at Oakleigh. Both of Irwin's sons fought in the Civil War. After the Civil War, his eldest son, Thomas, who had been an aide to Jefferson Davis, eventually became president of the Mobile Cotton Exchange.

After Alfred Irwin died, Thomas and his wife, Mary Anna Ketchum Irwin, took possession of Oakleigh. As the Irwins' fortunes rose, they began making additions to the house, including a west wing and a bathroom. They carried on the tradition set by Alfred and Margaret of hosting "high society" parties. Future U.S. president James Garfield is said to have drunk his first mint julep on Oakleigh's front porch in 1877. The last member of the Irwin family who lived in Oakleigh was Daisy Irwin Clisby, Alfred's granddaughter.

Oakleigh had several different owners in the twentieth century. Following General Irwin's death in 1911, his daughter, Daisy Irwin Clisby, sold Oakleigh to Dr. and Mrs. Herbert Cole. The Cole family was forced to repair the house in 1916 following a hurricane. Although they altered the interior of the house, they preserved the exterior's original appearance. Mrs. Cole also designed Oakleigh's sunken garden. The next owners were Mr. and Mrs. Denniston, who sold Oakleigh to the Hellenic American Progressive

Association. Oakleigh became the Greek Youth Center in the late 1940s until Mrs. Suzanne Robinson Gwynn purchased the old house in 1948 and converted it back to a family home. After living there for a few years, Mrs. Gwynn sold Oakleigh to the City of Mobile, which leased it to the Historic Mobile Preservation Society. Oakleigh is now operated as a house museum.

Marilyn Culpepper, the former director of the Historic Mobile Preservation Society, heard several eerie stories about the old house while serving as a docent there. One of the stories concerns several antique chairs that seem to have a mind of their own. She said, "There's the story about some chairs being moved in the second parlor. I'm pretty sure that a guide moved those chairs. In fact, I know she did it because she's a practical joker. This was the time the chairs moved on the anniversary of Daisy Irwin's death. I know that [incident] was bogus because we had a very superstitious house manager at the time who was very willing [to accept supernatural explanations for weird events]."

Although Marilyn is skeptical about the validity of some supposedly supernatural occurrences at Oakleigh, she cannot explain why several chairs moved on a different occasion. She explained, "The time the chairs were turned to face the fireplace was very interesting. These chairs were in the second parlor, and this is where all the activity seems to be focused." Marilyn is more willing to accept the possibility that ghosts moved the chairs this time because of her respect for the woman who served as the house manager at the time. She said, "This was a longtime employee, very stable. She went in early one morning to turn on the lights, and the chairs that normally sat on either side of the high marble table had been turned around to face the fireplace. It was as if someone had turned them to warm themselves by the fire. She questioned all the staff, and no one had touched the chairs. I really think that if someone had done it, they would have owned up to it. This incident is what gave the practical jokers the idea of moving the chairs [the second time]."

Apparently, the ghosts of Oakleigh manifest themselves visually on occasion. According to Marilyn Culpepper, one of the spirits is female: "Guests and tour guides have seen a woman in white walking down the hall outside the Batre bedroom. It might be an older child. People have also heard the rustle of petticoats when no one is there." Another shadowy figure who is occasionally glimpsed in the hallways is assumed to be male. "I've had guides and guests tell me that they've seen a man in a tail coat walking from the Batre bedroom through the hall," Marilyn said. The most common visual spirits, however, do not resemble human beings at all. "People have seen lights moving in the parlor at night when no one was there," Marilyn said. "That's pretty persistent. We hear that a lot."

Possibly the most memorable supernatural encounter at Oakleigh took place in 2000 when a family was taking the standard guided tour with a docent. Marilyn said:

> *They went into the foyer—no problem. They entered the first parlor—no problem. Then they came to the second parlor, and the child stopped. He did not want to enter the room. This is the room we call the Lobear Parlor because the Lobear portrait collection is in that room. His mother asked her son why he would not walk into the parlor, and he replied, "The lady does not want me to go in there." His mother said, "OK" and asked the docent if she and her son could step out of the parlor. The tour guide asked her if she wanted to leave the tour. "No," she replied, "we just don't want to go into this room." The boy and his mother bypassed the second parlor, walked down the hallway and visited the other rooms in the house. The docent, concerned about the boy's health, asked his mother if he was all right. "Well, he's a sensitive," she replied, "and he has had experiences before, and if he says he doesn't want to go someplace, we don't make him."*

Marilyn, who knew the boy's mother, talked to her afterward and asked her about the incident. The woman told Marilyn that "there was a woman in Oakleigh who did not like the second parlor because there was another woman in there that she despised." Intrigued by the woman's remarks, Marilyn walked into the parlor and was drawn to Thomas Sully's portrait of Margaret Kilshaw Irwin, the woman who saved Oakleigh by flying the Union Jack from the front porch.

Marilyn Culpepper is convinced that the boy's uneasy feeling about the second parlor has revealed the identity of Oakleigh's ghost. She explained, "Now, the folklore that surrounds Oakleigh is that there is a female ghost. We have always called her 'Miss Daisy.' I don't think that's true because Daisy didn't die in the house." Marilyn suspects that the ghost is the spirit of Daisy's mother, Mary Ketchum Irwin. "I think that if I was the hostess of that house, and there was a room dedicated to a woman who never lived there, who entertained Yankees during the occupation, and we had a big, huge Thomas Sully portrait of that woman, I think that's why she doesn't like that room."

ARKANSAS

BEBE

Arkansas State University

Arkansas State University (ASU) was founded in 1927 as the Junior Agricultural School of Central Arkansas. The university operated under four different names until becoming Arkansas State University–Bebe in 2001. Today, ASU combines academics with vocational training in technical fields. ASU–Bebe has expanded to include technical campuses in Newport and Searcy. Princess Hall on ASU's flagship campus is now used as a storage for the university's IT equipment. Sometimes, though, students encounter ghostly reminders of the building's past use as a women's dormitory.

The source of the haunting at Princess Hall dates back to April 1987. A twenty-one-year-old woman named Sandra Williams was on her way to visit her boyfriend in Quitman when she decided to make a quick stop at her dorm room in Princess Hall. After leaving the dormitory, Sandra disappeared. Several days later, her abandoned car was found near Romance, Arkansas. Sandra's badly decomposed corpse was found three miles from her car. A forensic investigation revealed that Sandra had been stabbed four times with a hunting knife.

Even though Sandra was not murdered on campus, her spirit appears to have returned to her old dorm room. A great deal of paranormal activity has been reported on the second floor where she lived. Students have walked into cold spots in the hallway. Doors have slammed shut on their own. One night, students heard someone running and screaming down the hall. A student was sound sleep when something nudged her awake. A few moments later, she heard someone scratching on the desk. Another student was trying to study when someone tried to force the door open. By the time she got to the door, no one was there. Sandra, it appears, is trying to show that she is still around—not in body but in spirit.

Hot Springs

Mayberry Inn

David Mayberry brought his family and servants to Garland County from Tennessee in 1832. At first, his family lived in a log cabin. Then in 1851, Mayberry built a much larger house on the other side of the Hot Springs–Fort Smith highway. His intention was to capitalize on the nearby springs, which were highly prized by the local Indians for their curative powers. The lower floor of the house was divided into two rooms, one for men and the other for women. Each room had a wooden tub filled with spring water. Mayberry and his family lived in the rest of the house.

Mayberry's business venture was a great success in the 1850s, primarily because his inn was situated midway between Mount Ida and Hot Springs. In addition, this part of Arkansas was rich in minerals. Consequently, a large number of prospectors and miners spent the night at the inn as they traveled to and from their claims. Fervently devoted to the Southern cause, Mayberry took a break from business during the Civil War and served in the Confederate army. He was wounded sixteen times but miraculously survived his wounds. His neighbors believed that he contracted blood poisoning from the Minié balls in his body and eventually went insane as a result. People said that toward the end of his life, Mayberry could be seen burying his gold and then digging it up the next night to prevent thieves from finding it. David Mayberry died in 1881. In 1892, prominent Hot Springs attorney Elias William Rector purchased the inn from the Mayberry family and turned it into a summer home. Today, the property is still owned by the descendants of Elias William Rector, but it is leased out to Mike Tripp, who plans to renovate the dilapidated old building.

David Mayberry's memory is preserved in the ghost legends people still tell about the Mayberry Inn. One of the stories passed down for generations concerns the Mayberry Inn's clientele. Supposedly, a band of outlaws began barging into rooms and robbing and murdering the guests, some of whom had struck it rich in the mines. The outlaws were so brutal that they even murdered guests because they had no money. For years, people said that the bloodstains in one of the "murder rooms" resisted all attempts at removal. In frustration, David Mayberry painted the floor brown to mask the bloodstains.

David Mayberry himself is the subject of many of the inn's ghost stories. The story goes that after going mad from blood poisoning, Mayberry stabbed his wife and buried her in the fireplace. People say that her cries can be heard inside the inn at midnight. According to one of the variants of the tale, Mayberry drowned his infant son after murdering his wife. For years, people have heard cries coming from the bathtub in the basement.

JONESBORO

Keller's Chapel Cemetery

Keller's Chapel Cemetery is located on Keller's Chapel Road off Southwest Drive behind Keller's Chapel. The chapel and the cemetery were founded by Uriah and Julia Keller, who moved to Jonesboro from South Carolina in the 1850s. Keller's Chapel Cemetery is one of the oldest cemeteries in Craighead County. Over two hundred local residents are buried here, including veterans of the Civil War and the Spanish-American War. Many of the people interred in the cemetery have been long forgotten. In fact, most of the people who visit the cemetery today are teenagers looking to make contact with Jonesboro's past.

Many people claim to have had paranormal experiences inside Keller's Chapel Cemetery. Legend has it that the sound of babies crying inside the cemetery has been heard. Some people claim to have seen the ghosts of children who are buried there. Fiery rings have been seen inside the cemetery. Teenagers who have turned off their cars at the gates have been unable to start their engines again for several hours.

At the time of this writing, only one of the cemetery's legends has been debunked. Dustine Faber, a reporter for the *ASU Herald*, says that many visitors claim to have seen a red light flashing on one of the tombstones in the cemetery. Faber walked through the cemetery and discovered that a light from a radio tower reflects off one of the tombstones. Faber believes that if the cemetery is actually haunted, the ghost is probably the spirit of W.M. Hamilton, whose birthdate—June 15, 1856—has been etched on his tombstone but not his day of death.

LITTLE ROCK

The Old State House

The Old State House was built between 1833 and 1842. It had been commissioned by John Pope, the territorial governor. Union troops occupied the building during the Civil War. After the new capitol building was constructed in 1912, a medical school was housed in the Old State House. It was converted into a museum by the General Assembly in 1947. The building was renovated in 1996 and was designated a National Historic Landmark. Today, the Old State House is one of the most historic—and haunted—buildings in Little Rock.

The activity inside the Old State House was generated by two violent incidents that occurred there. The earliest of these events occurred in 1837, when Speaker of the House John Wilson ruled a representative named Anthony as being "out of order." Anthony had just argued with Wilson shortly before, and he pulled out a knife. Wilson did the same, and the two men commenced fighting. Within a few harrowing minutes, Anthony lay in a pool of blood, taking his last few breaths. Many staff members claim to have seen Wilson's ghost, dressed in a frock coat.

Some believe that the wandering spirit in the Old State House is the ghost of someone else. Seventeen months after Elisha Baxter was declared the winner of the governor's race, he was challenged by his opponent, Joseph Brooks, who accused Baxter of cheating. Brooks had Baxter removed from the building. He then had a cannon placed in front of the Old State House to keep Baxter's supporters at bay. Meanwhile, Baxter set up a temporary office just down the street. Baxter and Brooks vied for control of Arkansas until President Ulysses S. Grant intervened and named Baster the rightful governor of Arkansas. Many people believe that Brooks haunts the Old State House because he has still not recovered from being ousted as governor. His ghost, they say, is the one that creates the cold spots in the old building and places a cold hand on people's shoulders. Of course, it is also possible that two ghosts—the spirits of John Wilson and Joseph Brooks—are making their presence known in the Old State House.

SEARCY

Harding University

Harding University first came into being in 1924 with the merger of Arkansas Christian College and Harper College. The college derived its name from the co-founder of Nashville Bible School in Nashville, Tennessee. Harding College was relocated from Morrilton, Arkansas, to Searcy, Arkansas, in 1934 on the campus of Galloway College, a Methodist Episcopal school for girls. Galloway College is no more, but the legend of "Galloway Gertie" lives on.

At the turn of the century, Galloway College enjoyed a reputation as one of the finest institutions in the South for young upper-class women. Godden Hall, the women's dormitory, was described by a professor at Harding College as a forbidding, Gothic-looking structure. In the early 1920s, a young woman named Gertrude returned to Godden Hall from a party she had attended with her boyfriend. After saying goodnight to her date, she walked into the dormitory and did her best to muffle the rustling of her white evening gown. She had almost reached her room when she heard a noise in the vicinity of the elevator, so she turned around to investigate. A few minutes later, the girls on her floor were awakened by a piercing scream. The dorm mother called the police, who discovered the body of "Gertie Sue," as she was known to her friends, at the bottom of the elevator shaft. One of the girls swore she saw a dark figure run away from the elevator. Despite the suspicious circumstances, Gertrude's death was deemed an accident by the police. She was buried in the same white evening gown she died in.

Like the spirits of many victims whose murderers were never caught, Gertrude's ghost cannot find peace. For decades, students reported seeing the specter of a woman in a white dress floating across the campus grounds. The most famous sighting was recorded in the November 4, 1950 issue of the student newspaper, the *Bison*. One night, a student living in the dormitory woke up and walked down the hallway to get a drink. As she walked past the partially boarded-up elevator, her curiosity drove her to peer through the crack in the boards. There, inside the elevator, was a beautiful blond girl in a white evening gown. The frightened girl screamed and ran back to her room. She woke up her roommate and urged her to take a look inside the elevator. Her roommate walked to the elevator and was so terrified by what she saw that she backed up against the opposite wall and mumbled, "She walked out of the elevator and right through the wall."

Godden Hall was razed in 1951, and the bricks were used to build the Pattie Cobb Women's residence hall and the Claude Rogers Lee Music Center. In recent years, a great deal of paranormal activity has been reported inside the music building, including the sounds of ghostly footsteps and the faint strains of piano music. Some students and staff believe that the strange figure that has been seen looking down from an upper window in the music building is the tragic spirit of Gertie Sue, still looking for justice.

FLORIDA

PENSACOLA

Noble Manor Bed and Breakfast

The house that is now the Noble Manor Bed and Breakfast was built at 110 West Strong Street by an ex-Confederate soldier in 1905. The Tudor Revival house was designed by Charlie Hill Turner. The wooden furnishings in the house, including the entrance hall staircase and the restored heart pine floors, recall Florida's timber boom days around the turn of the century. Beginning in the 1940s, the old building served as a boardinghouse for men. Originally, the house had five bedrooms upstairs and four bedrooms downstairs. In the early 1970s, the first of a series of families purchased the boardinghouse and added their own distinctive touches. When Bonnie Robertson and her husband bought the house in 2005, a Coke machine and an old couch were sitting on the front porch. After renovating their new home, the Robertsons opened the Noble Manor Bed and Breakfast. Today, their home is one of the best-preserved houses in Pensacola's North Hill Historic District. It is also one of the most haunted.

The Robertsons' housekeeper claims to have seen a female ghost in the house a number of times, usually in the hallway at the side of the stairs on the first floor and in the hallway on the second floor. One day, she was standing on the first floor when she sensed someone walking behind her. She called out Bonnie's name but got no response. Later, she asked Bonnie, "Didn't you hear me call your name?" Bonnie replied, "I wasn't even in the house at the time." One morning in the late 2000s, the housekeeper was working in the kitchen when she decided to walk over to a closet in the kitchen hallway. She was surprised to find that she was unable to open the door all the way. Later, she told Bonnie that it seemed as if someone was pulling on the doorknob from inside the closet. Interestingly enough, the Robertsons' dog refuses to walk down this particular hallway.

A guest who stayed in the Tribeca Room on the second floor with her husband in 2009 also had a personal encounter with a ghost in the house. One morning, she walked into the bathroom across the hall, shut the door and prepared to take a shower. Immediately, she heard someone turning the doorknob from the outside. Thinking that it was her husband, she exclaimed, "I'm in here!" When her husband did not reply, she opened the door. No one was there. Perplexed, she went back to her bedroom and asked her husband if he had tried to get into the bathroom. He said that he had been in the bedroom the entire time.

A few months later, another female guest had a strange experience in the same bathroom. She was washing her hands when she smelled smoke. Thinking that there might be a short in the wiring, she ran down the stairs and told the owners about the smell. They went upstairs but could not find any trace of a fire in the bathroom. Later that day, the Robertsons called in an electrician to check out the wiring. He said that he could find nothing wrong.

On July 8, 2010, my wife, Marilyn, and I spent the night at Noble Manor Bed and Breakfast. At 9:25 p.m., she was lying in bed, and I was sitting in a chair, watching television. All at once, Marilyn said that she smelled smoke. By the time I rose from my chair and walked over to the bed, the smell had dissipated. At breakfast the next morning, Bonnie told us that a couple of years earlier, a contractor had detected an apple smell in the same room. The contractor's brother, who had just recently died, was fond of smoking apple tobacco. Apparently, the brother's spirit utilized this familiar smell to assure the contractor that everything was all right.

Over the years, investigators have confirmed Bonnie's suspicions that her house might be haunted. In 2009, a local ghost-hunting group captured a large number of orbs with their digital cameras. That same year, a guest who was a psychic informed Bonnie that she felt the presence of two female spirits in the house. However, Bonnie, who has lived in the house for five years, has not seen anything paranormal. She said, "I have sat downstairs in the dark parlor late at night waiting for guests quite a few times. That would be a good time for ghosts to show up, but they never have."

Old Sacred Heart Hospital

On September 15, 1915, the Daughters of Charity opened the first Catholic hospital in Pensacola at 1010 North Twelfth Avenue. Pensacola Hospital, as it was known back then, was built in one year by Evans Brothers Construction of Birmingham, Alabama, at a cost of $400,000. The building was designed by an Austrian immigrant named A.O. Von Herbulis. This huge Gothic Revival structure has eighty-six thousand square feet of floor space and over five hundred casement windows. Other distinctive touches include the battlement at the parapet and the Tudor-style wooden entry doors, which are repeated in doorways throughout the building.

Pensacola Hospital was indeed a welcome addition to the community because it had the first bacterial, surgical, therapeutic and radiological facilities in the entire state. The nuns lived up to their order's motto—"service to all"—by devoting the third level of the east wing to the treatment of African American and Creole patients. In 1948, the name of the hospital was changed to Sacred Heart Hospital of Pensacola in accordance with the wishes of Mother Margaret O'Keefe. The old building was vacated in 1965 when the hospital moved to North Ninth Avenue. Four years later, a private school for liberal arts began holding classes in the old building. When the school closed in 1978, the building stood abandoned for two years. Then in March 1980, the old hospital was purchased by Tower East, an investment group owned by B. Neal Armstrong and Stephen F. Ritz. Ritz's family spent years cleaning up the old hospital. Using historic photographs as a guide, the new owners' restoration efforts succeeded in preserving the hospital's historical integrity. On February 16, 1982, the Old Sacred Heart Hospital became the only hospital in the panhandle to be added to the U.S. National Register of Historic Places.

Today, the Old Sacred Heart Hospital is an office building and the site of a number of small businesses. Several restaurants—Madison's Diner, O'Zone Pizza Pub and Et Café—are located on the first floor. The lower levels are also home to a yoga studio, a veterinary clinic, a Montessori school, several private offices and a local theater company, the Loblolly Theater. Tours are given in parts of the old hospital Monday through Friday from 8:00 a.m. to 5:00 p.m.

For most of its fifty years as a hospital, Old Sacred Heart Hospital was said to be haunted by the ghost of a nun. She was a kindly spirit who often approached other nuns as they crossed a particular hallway on their way to the hospital's chapel. Over the years, many nuns reported feeling someone tap them on the back of the shoulders. Nuns who had been working in Old Sacred Hospital for years identified the spirit as the ghost of a kindly old nun who, in life, had often touched people on the shoulders to get their attention.

Because the building has had very few structural changes in its history, the exterior stonework still retains its Gothic appearance. Not surprisingly, the Old Sacred Heart Hospital has been used as the setting for a number of horror films produced by the Florida State University film school, including *3 a.m.* (2003) and *Lamia* (2004), which has won a number of awards in film festivals across the country. Few people today realize that the Old Sacred Heart Hospital is much more than a "pretend" haunted building.

St. Augustine

Kenwood Inn

Kenwood Inn is unusual among many bed-and-breakfasts in the South in that it was converted from an antebellum house or mansion. It first opened as an inn in 1865. In 1885, an addition was made to the side of the inn, and it became the LaBorde Boarding House. In 1910, a wing was added to the back of the building. Through the years, the inn has been operated under several names, including the Marine Street Inn and the Kenwood Hotel. In 2008, the current owners, Pat and Ted Dubosz, purchased the old inn from Mark and Kerianne Constant. The paranormal activity that was rumored to have taken place when the Constants ran the inn continued under the new ownership.

The most haunted room in the Kenwood Inn is Room 7. A psychic who walked into the room informed Kerianne Constant that the room was haunted by a ghost named Raymond. He is most likely the spirit of Raymond LaBorde, who ran the inn in the 1880s. Many guests who stayed in the room reported that the lights went off and on during the night, and the water faucet turned on by itself. In his book *Ancient City Hauntings*, author Dave Lapham says that a woman who booked Room 7 told Mark Constant that she had heard about the ghost of Raymond and that she was hoping to encounter him. Later that day, she left her room to tour St. Augustine. When she returned, all three locks to the room were frozen. Some of the staff believed that Raymond had intentionally locked her out of his room.

Kenwood Inn is haunted by the spirit of Raymond LaBorde, who ran the inn in the 1880s. *Courtesy of the author.*

A woman sleeping in Room 8 was awakened by a ghostly cat that had climbed up on the bed. *Courtesy of the author.*

Michelle Davidson, author of *Florida's Haunted Hospitality*, said that a woman was awakened in the middle of the night by the sound of pages being turned in a book. Her sister told her the next morning that she had not been reading a book the previous night. Another guest in Room 7 said that in the morning, she found herself covered up by a comforter she had placed on a chair the night before.

The third floor is reputed to be haunted as well. David Lapham said that a woman staying in Room 17 was walking out the door when she saw the spirit of an elderly woman in a Victorian-era dress sitting in a chair. She was wearing her gray hair in a tight bun.

In an interview I conducted with Pat Dobosz in September 2013, she said that people sleeping on the second floor have complained about hearing furniture being moved around on the third floor while in Room 18. Pat said that a servant named Jasmine lived in that room in the 1920s. Pat continued, "She was the mistress of a local doctor. When she tried to get him to divorce his wife and marry her, he killed her on the third floor." A medium who was visiting the inn told Pat that Jasmine was Native American. A few weeks before my visit, a couple who was staying in Room 18 abruptly left in the middle of the night with no explanation.

TALLAHASSEE

Goodwood Museum and Gardens

Hardy Croom was a lawyer, planter and amateur botanist who established a farm around Tallahassee in the 1830s. He is known today for the discovery of rare tree that he found growing in Bristol, Florida, in 1834. Croom contacted botanist Dr. John Torrey at Columbia College. Torrey declared the tree a species that once grew worldwide before the last ice age. Croom believed that these were the fabled gopherwood trees in the Bible that supplied the wood for Noah's ark. The scientific name for these trees, which are found only in Bristol, is *Torreyan taxifolia*.

In 1835, Hardy Croom began building a magnificent home for himself; his wife, Frances; and their children. He named the house Goodwood. In October 1837, he was bringing the family back from North Carolina on the steamship SS *Home*. The ship was lost in a terrible storm, and

Croom and his family drowned. Hardy's brother, Bryan, and his wife, Eveline Croom, inherited Goodwood. Bryan immediately set about completing the main house. He also planted cotton, corn and sweet potatoes. However, Bryan and Eveline soon became embroiled in a lawsuit with Frances Croom's mother, Henrietta Smith. After a court battle that lasted twenty years, Mrs. Smith won and sold the house to Arvah and Susan Hopkins, who turned the house into the social center of Tallahassee between the 1850s and 1880s. In 1865, after the Union army captured Tallahassee, the Hopkins reluctantly entertained Federal officers in their home.

Following the death of her husband in 1885, Mrs. Hopkins sold Goodwood to an Englishman, Dr. William Lamb Arrowsmith, and his wife, Elizabeth. Dr. Arrowsmith died within a few months of taking ownership of the estate, so Elizabeth occupied herself by planting beds of daffodils on the west lawn in front of the driveway. She also had a large arrow of paved bricks made in the ground. She wanted the arrow to point south to, in her words, "make people ponder."

Elizabeth Arrowsmith remained at Goodwood for twenty-five years before finally selling it in 1911 to Fanny Tiers, the wealthy widow of Alexander Tiers. Fanny Tiers, whose principal estate was in Morris County, New Jersey, immediately set about expanding the estate. She built several guest cottages on the estate and a large swimming pool. She also had a water tank constructed in the backyard. Gravitational flow provided water for the faucets and toilets. Fanny was also responsible for the general Colonial Revival design of the gardens. Because Goodwood was one of the first homes in Tallahassee to have electric lights, large crowds formed around the house whenever Fanny turned on the lights at night.

In 1925, Margaret Hodges, the wife of Senator William C. Hodges, sent her husband to Goodwood to buy an antique bed. Fanny refused to sell the bed separately, but she did agree to sell Hodges the house and all the furnishings, including the bed. During parties that the senator and his wife held at Goodwood, he often remarked that this was the most expensive bed in Florida. Hodges also bought back some of the original furniture that had been sold by some of the previous owners to pay their legal bills. One of William Hodges's pet projects was the expansion of the garden. All of the plants in the garden today are taken from Hodges's 1929 inventory. In a high-profile trial in 1930, William Hodges defended a local woman named Dixie Goad for the murder of her husband.

In 1940, Senator Hodges died, but Margaret continued to entertain at her luxurious home. One of the guests who visited Goodwood was the renowned writer Helen Keller. In 1948, Margaret married one of the men who rented one of her guest cottages, an army officer named Thomas M. Hood. He was an artist who painted the daisies, roses and grapes on the ceilings and walls of the house. By the 1970s, the house was becoming increasingly difficult to maintain, but Margaret insisted that Goodwood was "too precious to part with." She passed away in 1978. Before his death in 1990, Thomas M. Hood established the Margaret E. Wilson Foundation in memory of his wife to preserve Goodwood. Today, Goodwood Museum and Gardens, Inc., has assumed stewardship of Goodwood.

Although Goodwood is known primarily as one of the most beautiful historic homes in Tallahassee, it is gradually becoming known among paranormal enthusiasts as a very haunted place as well. In her book *Hauntings in Florida's Panhandle*, author Nicole Carlson Easley chronicled some of the ghostly activity that has occurred inside the old house. Easley said that volunteers who stand in front of the fireplace in the dining room have felt the unmistakable presence of someone standing directly behind them. Docents and guests have experienced sudden drops of temperature while walking through parts of the house. Volunteers who were cataloguing items inside the house one day reported feeling very cold when they picked up specific objects. Goodwood, it seems, is a place where the previous owners still make claim to their property, even from the "other side."

The Knott House

Luella and William Knott were one of Tallahassee's most prominent couples in the first half of the twentieth century. Luella, who was born in Graham, North Carolina, on May 31, 1871, became an orphan at age six following the death of her parents from tuberculosis. She graduated from Greensboro Methodist College in 1891. Her husband, William Knott, was born in Terrell County, Georgia, on November 24, 1863. While growing up, William helped his father in the family's citrus grove near Leesburg. As an adult, William partnered with his brother Charles and started a phosphate mining business near Ocala. Later, William enjoyed success as an accountant and a civil servant.

William met Luella in central Florida, where she was teaching school. The couple was married in 1895 and moved to Tallahassee two years later.

At the time, William was working as the state financial agent. He became the state's first auditor under Governor Jennings's administration. When Sidney Catts became governor in 1917, William returned to agriculture. He also accepted the position of head administrator of the state hospital in Chattahoochee. In 1927, William was once again appointed state auditor under Governor John Martin.

Because William was working for the state once again, he and Luella returned to Tallahassee. In 1928, they moved into the house that is now the Knott House Museum. A year later, William replaced John Luning as state treasurer and held that position under two more governors. He retired at age seventy-five.

At the same time that William was building his political career, Luella occupied herself as a mother, poet and social activist. When she was not homeschooling the couple's three children, she found time to lead a campaign against the consumption of alcohol in Florida. Because she was the wife of an important state official, Luella felt obligated to entertain at her home. She frequently tied her poems to the furnishings during these parties to attract her guests' attention to her antiques. Luella died on April 11, 1965; her husband had preceded her in death only eight days earlier.

Luella and William were not the only occupants of the house at 301 East Park Avenue. George Proctor built the house in 1843 for a lawyer named Thomas Hagner, who presented it as a wedding gift to his wife, Catherine Gamble. Following her husband's death two years later, Catherine turned the home into a boardinghouse. In 1865, toward the end of the Civil War, Brigadier General Edward McCook read the Emancipation Proclamation from the porch. Dr. George Betton purchased the house in 1883. He set up a clinic in the basement of the house. Following Dr. Betton's death in the house in 1896, another doctor, Dr. John W. Scott, moved into the house with his wife, Caroline Scott, in 1919. He died in the house in 1920, eight years before Luella and William Knott moved in.

The last person to live in the Knott House was Luella and William's son, Charlie. He inherited the house in 1965 following his parents' deaths and remained there until his death in 1985. A year later, the house was acquired by the Tallahassee Preservation Board, which operated it as a museum. It was opened to the public in 1992.

Because so many people have died in the Knott House, it is small wonder that locals find it easy to believe that it is haunted. A photograph depicting what appears to be the ghostly image of a person is on display inside the house. It was taken by one of the staff members. In her book *Hauntings in Florida's Panhandle*, author Nicole Carlson Easley says that a staff member who was working in her office late one evening heard someone walking up and down the stairs. She became frightened when she realized that the young woman she was working with had gone home for the day. Several staff members have heard someone walking around the second floor when it was supposed to be empty.

Visitors to the Knott House have also had some very strange encounters. Visitors participating in the museum's "Real Ghost House" tour have reported walking into parts of the old house that are unusually cold. A few guests have sensed large amounts of psychic energy emanating from the bookcase. A visitor claimed to have caught a glimpse of a male apparition in one of the upper bedrooms of the house. According to author Nicole Carlson Easley, one guest claimed to have seen a group of women wearing antebellum dresses in the living room. They may have been the spirits of some of Luella's friends, who often wore nineteenth-century dresses during specific social functions. The legacy of Luella and William Knox, it seems, is of the ethereal as well as the material kind.

The Lively Building

Constructed in 1875 at 200 South Monroe Street, the Lively Building is one of the city's most historic structures. Its name is derived from Matthew Lively, a pharmacist who operated a drugstore on the first floor. The top floor was used as offices. The Lively Building acquired a somewhat notorious reputation when the Leon Bar opened up on the first floor in 1892.

Many of the Leon Bar's customers were a rowdy bunch of cowboys known as the Florida Crackers. These nomadic cowboys, who could trace their lineage back to the Scotch-Irish and English settlers, made their livings working the Pineywoods cattle that roamed the Florida woods. These free-ranging cows were descended from the hardy breed of cattle left behind by the Spanish explorers in the fifteenth and sixteenth centuries. They thrived in the wilds of Florida because of their natural resistance to the indigenous diseases and parasites. The Crackers, who were as tough as the cattle they drove, differed from the cowboys of the American Southwest in that they used cow whips and dogs instead of lassos to herd cattle. On payday, a large number of these men could be found "whooping it up" at the Leon Bar, where they drank beer and whiskey and cavorted with loose women. Shootings and stabbings were common occurrences at this Wild West–type saloon. An untold number of people are said to have been murdered there.

The Leon Bar was closed in 1904—not by the local police but by a local ordinance prohibiting the sale of liquor within the city limits. Tallahassee was one of many cities that were affected by the temperance movement, which encouraged moderation or the prohibition of alcoholic spirits. The temperance movement was driven mostly by women, most notably Susan B. Anthony, Frances E. Willard and Carry A. Nation. Temperance workers described saloons like the Leon Bar as "enticing [places] where our boys may drink in style and elegance amidst strains of dreamy music and all that gilds and sugarcoats sin." The efforts of the temperance movement eventually resulted in government regulation of alcohol and the passing of the Eighteenth Amendment.

The Leon Bar is long gone, and so are the Florida Crackers, whose freewheeling lifestyle could not resist the encroachments of civilization.

Ghostly cowboys, known locally as "Crackers," have been sighted around the entrance to the Lively Building. *Courtesy of the author.*

The Pineywoods cattle that supplied them with a living have been placed on the "critical" list by the American Livestock Breeds Conservancy. However, some people say that the spirits of these free-spirited cowboys are still "whooping it up" at the former saloon. Apparitions of lanky, bearded young men wearing leather chaps and wide-brimmed hats have been sighted lounging around the corner where the bright lights of the Leon Bar once beckoned to thirsty souls eager to spend their hard-earned money and forget about the rigors of their lives for a while.

GEORGIA

SAVANNAH

Bonaventure Cemetery

Bonaventure Cemetery is not only one of the most famous graveyards in the United States, but it is also one of the most beautiful. The story goes that a fine mansion, the home of Mary and Josiah Tattnall, once stood on this tract of land. Legend has it that the massive oaks were planted in the shape of a letter "M" entwined with the letter "T." Following the Revolutionary War, their son, Josiah Tattnall Jr., became master of the plantation. Josiah was a gregarious man and great host who became known for the extravagant parties he threw at the mansion. The last of these parties was held one fateful night in November 1800. At the height of the revelry, a servant whispered in Josiah's ear that the house was on fire. Josiah is said to have ordered the servants to move all of the furniture out on the front lawn. He then asked his guests to join him outside. In the glare of the flames that consumed the mansion, Josiah and his guests toasted the grand old mansion that had been the site of so many fine parties in years gone by. They then threw their glasses against one of the oak trees. Some people say that on late autumn nights, one can still hear ghostly laughter, as well as the tinkle of glass and silverware.

This is the oldest—but by no means the only—legend that has been generated at Bonaventure Cemetery. The first interments at the cemetery

Bonaventure Cemetery, Savannah, Georgia. *Courtesy of the Library of Congress.*

were Josiah Tattnall, his wife and their four sons. The graveyard was incorporated as a cemetery in 1869. Irish playwright Oscar Wilde visited the cemetery in the late nineteenth century and called it "incomparable." The cemetery's most famous residents are poet Conrad Aiken and composer Johnny Mercer, who is said to have been inspired by the nearby Wilmington River to write "Moon River." Naturalist John Muir spent a week in the cemetery, even going so far as to sleep on top of the graves, despite the stories that locals had told him about the spirits of the graveyard.

Many of these stories revolve around the magnificent statues that enhance the cemetery's eerie atmosphere. A number of statues are said to have some disturbingly real facial expressions. Some visitors swear that the statue of a young woman named Corinne smiles at people she is particularly attracted to. Others claim to have heard the giggling of children and the crying of a baby inside the cemetery.

A pack of wild dogs nicknamed "hell hounds" is even rumored to have made the old cemetery its home. Although the fierce canines have never actually been seen inside the cemetery, some visitors claim to have felt their hot breaths on the backs of their legs. Others claim to have heard their spectral howling late at night.

Bonaventure's most famous ghost legend concerns a child named "Little Gracie." Born in 1883, she was the daughter of the manager of the Pulaski Hotel. After she died in 1890, her parents hired a prominent sculptor named John Walz to carve a fitting monument for their beloved daughter. Using a photograph, Walz created an amazing likeness of the little girl, which has been enthralling visitors to Bonaventure Cemetery for over a century. Visitors leave toys and coins at Gracie's grave, especially at Christmastime. People say that she cries when the objects are removed from her grave. Some of the more imaginative of the cemetery's visitors wonder if the fence surrounding Little Gracie's grave was placed there to protect the monument from vandalism or to keep Little Gracie locked inside. Interest in Bonaventure Cemetery soared after the publication of John Berendt's 1994 novel *Midnight in the Garden of Good and Evil*, which recounts a number of the site's legends. The stately cemetery that had been favored by locals as a picturesque spot for picnics and evening strolls is now attracting people who "haunt" the graveyard to see if there is any truth to the ghost stories that have been told about Bonaventure Cemetery for centuries.

Fort Pulaski

Fort Pulaski was constructed by the Army Corps of Engineers between 1843 and 1847 on a marshy strip of land called Cockrell Island. It required a series of foundation pilings to be driven seventy feet into the ground. The masonry fort consists of over 25 million "Savanna Gray" and "Rose Red" bricks. By 1860, only twenty guns had been installed in the fort, so the 134 Savannah Confederate volunteers under the command of Colonel Charles H. Olmstead had no trouble capturing the fort in 1861. However, a year later, Union forces under the command of General David Hunter landed at Tybee Island with the intention of pummeling Fort Pulaski with thirty-six pieces of artillery. The bombardment began on April 10, 1862, and ended the next day with the surrender of Colonel Olmstead's troops.

In 1864, 550 Confederate soldiers were held prisoner at Fort Pulaski. Because food was scarce, the prisoners had to subsist on rats, cats and kittens. Thirteen Confederate soldiers died at Fort Pulaski of dehydration and starvation. Because the advent of rifled-bore cannons had spelled the end of masonry forts, the military was reluctant to make improvements to Fort Pulaski after the Civil War. In 1880, Fort Pulaski was decommissioned and left to the elements, even though it was still owned by the War

Department. Federal troops were stationed at Fort Pulaski briefly in 1898 during the Spanish-American War, but it was abandoned once again when fighting ceased.

On October 15, 1924, President Calvin Coolidge saved Fort Pulaski from further deterioration by designating the old fort as a National Monument. In 1933, Fort Pulaski was transferred from the War Department to the Department of the Interior. Between 1998 and 1999, Fort Pulaski's cemetery was rediscovered.

Fort Pulaski became known as a haunted site not long after its transfer to the Department of the Interior. Some visitors have sensed an unseen presence standing near them. Others have heard a spectral voice calling their names. The ghosts of Confederate and Union soldiers have been seen standing guard both inside and outside the fort. Disembodied footsteps have been heard in the grass outside the fort. A number of visitors have "uneasy" feelings on the stairway. Legend has it that a casualty of the 1862 bombardment was carried down the stairs. In several parts of the fort, including Colonel Olmstead's room, visitors have been overcome with a sense of despair.

The most famous sighting at Fort Pulaski occurred in the late 1980s during the filming of scenes for the Civil War movie *Glory* in Savannah. A group of reenactors, who were featured in the climactic battle scene, decided to visit Fort Pulaski in their spare time. They were walking through the casements and across the parade ground when they were approached by a young man wearing a Confederate lieutenant's uniform. He upbraided the reenactors for not saluting him when they passed by and ordered them to fall into formation. He then told them face about (i.e., turn around). In a few seconds, the soldier was gone. For some of the men, their re-creation of the past had become a bit too real.

COLUMBUS

The Springer Opera House

By May 1870, Frances Springer, an immigrant from Alsace, had finalized plans to construct a theater at the corner of Crawford and Ogelthorpe Streets. The Springer Opera House held its grand opening on February 21,

The Springer Opera House, Columbus, Georgia. *Courtesy of the Library of Congress.*

1871. Over the years, a number of celebrated performers have appeared at the Springer Opera House, including Ethel Barrymore, Lilly Langtry, Agnes de Mille, Will Rogers, William Jennings Bryan, Franklin D. Roosevelt and John Phillips Sousa. However, Edwin Booth, the actor brother of John Wilkes Booth, is the most famous actor who has ever performed at the Springer Opera House—probably because he is rumored to have never left.

In the mid-nineteenth century, Edwin, John and their father, Junius Brutus Booth, were part of America's premier theatrical family. Still, the three men appeared in only one play together: Shakespeare's *Julius Caesar*. Edwin, who was an avowed Unionist, disapproved of his younger brother's Southern sympathies. Following the assassination of Abraham Lincoln in 1865, the Booth family went into seclusion. In 1876, Booth appeared in his celebrated role as Hamlet at the Springer Opera House, which was only five years old at the time. Edwin's warm reception at Columbus was an important step in rebuilding his career. Legend has it that before he left Columbus, Edwin vowed that he would return to the Springer Opera House after his death and remain there until another performance of *Hamlet* was staged.

Edwin's ghost has also been blamed for some of the poltergeist-like activity in the theater, such as those times when props malfunction. A number of visitors say that doors to the smaller upper balconies have opened by themselves, even though this part of the theater is no longer used. A group of people who were standing near the portrait of Edwin Booth that hangs in the lobby were facing the bar when one of three wine bottles sitting on the bar tipped over by itself.

In 1971, Governor Jimmy Carter named the Springer Opera House the State Theater of Georgia in honor of its 100th anniversary. Six years later, the Springer Opera House was designated a National Historic Landmark. However, the Springer is best known in the paranormal community as one of the most haunted theaters in the United States.

Dahlonega

Stonepile Gap

Historic markers have become an indelible part of the landscape along roadways in the South. One of the strangest markers stands at a pile of rocks just north of Dahlonega. According to legend, this is the grave of a lovely young Cherokee girl named Trahlyta. Supposedly, she was told by the mountain medicine man that she would become even more beautiful if she would drink from Porter Springs and plead with the spirits never to grow old. Before long, she became known as one of the most beautiful women in the entire Cherokee tribe. Unfortunately, word of Trahlyta's breathtaking beauty soon reached the ears of a Cherokee warrior named Wahsega. She had rejected him as a suitor once before, and now that she had become famous for her beauty, he wanted her even more. One day, he abducted Trahlyta and took her home with him, where she became a virtual prisoner. After a few weeks, the poor girl started to waste away. Just before she died, she asked Wahsega to bury her on her beloved mountain. As she was drawing her last breath, Trahlyta said, "Strangers as they pass by may drop a stone on my grave, and they, too, shall be young and happy, as I once was."

For many years, both Cherokees and whites have placed stones on Trahlyta's grave for good luck. Even today, most people passing by the intersection of U.S. 19 and S.R. 60 on Cedar Mountain treat the grave with respect. Apparently, Trahlyta is transformed from a benign spirit into a vengeful revenant when people try to desecrate her grave. On two occasions, workers attempted to relocate her grave during road construction. Both times, one of the workers died as he was trying to move the rocks. Any believer of the paranormal knows that there are dire consequences for those who do not respect the dying wishes of the dearly departed.

St. Simons Island

Christ Church Cemetery

Different nations have vied for control of St. Simons Island for five hundred years. When the Spanish explorers and missionaries arrived in the 1500s, they encountered the Guale Indians. In 1733, British soldiers came to St. Simons Island when James Ogelthorpe established Fort Frederica and Fort St. Simons there to protect Savannah. In 1742, during Ogelthorpe's attack against the Spanish in St. Augustine, the Spanish briefly regained control of St. Simons Island, but the British ultimately prevailed and took over the island once again. Soon, British planters and settlers began farming the area. Slaves were brought in to do most of the work. At the outbreak of the Civil War, Confederate troops brought in artillery to protect the island—and Savannah—but left when an attack by Union forces was imminent. Today, St. Simons Island is a resort town that beckons vacationers to partake of the island's beauty and deep history. One of the island's most popular—and haunted—attractions is Christ Church.

Christ Church is part of the town of Frederica, which was eventually abandoned after the British army left the island. The only remnants of the early European settlement are Fort Frederica and Christ Church. Generations of planters are buried in Christ Church cemetery. One of these graves has become the focus of one of the island's signature ghost stories. According to one version of the tale, the husband of a woman who was buried there lit a candle on her grave every night. Locals said that even after her death, the flickering light was still visible. Another variant has it that a young woman who had been told ghost stories by her Caribbean nurse became so afraid of the dark that she devoted her adult life to candle-making. She eventually died from an untreated wax burn, and her spirit continues to illuminate her grave site.

Today, a wall surrounding Christ Church Cemetery has obstructed the view of the ghost light. However, the ghost story, like the light itself, shows no signs of fading away anytime soon.

St. Simons Lighthouse

In 1804, a plantation owner named John Couper sold a four-acre plot of land known as "Couper's Point" to the federal government for one dollar so that a lighthouse could be built there. Three years later, the Treasury Department hired James Gould to build the lighthouse and a keeper's house. The lighthouse, which was completed in 1808, was a seventy-five-foot pyramid-shaped structure made of brick and tabby. President James Madison appointed James Gould the first lighthouse keeper in 1810. Gould held this position until his retirement in 1837. In 1857, the iron lantern was replaced by a third-order, double-convex Fresnel lens. In 1862, the Confederate army destroyed the lighthouse to keep it out of the hands of Federal troops. After the Civil War, Charles Cluskey was hired by the U.S. government to build a second lighthouse west of the original lighthouse. The lighthouse was completed in 1872, even though Cluskey and some of the workers had died of malaria in 1871. In 1890, a brick oil house was built for the storage of kerosene oil. In 1934, the kerosene lamp was replaced by electricity. In 1953, the lighthouse became fully automated. The Department of the Interior acquired the lighthouse in 1960. In 2004, the lighthouse was deeded to the Coastal Georgia Historical Society.

Today, St. Simons Lighthouse is known as much for its ghost as it is for its history. The story goes that in 1880, lighthouse keeper Frederick Osborne angered his assistant over remarks he had made to Osborne's wife over dinner. Later that evening, the assistant shot Osborne. Stephens was charged with murder but was later acquitted.

Osborne, who was so dedicated that he climbed the tower as many three times a day, is said to still be on the job. Many people have heard his footsteps walking up and down the spiral staircase at night. Osborne's apparition has appeared on several occasions both in and around the tower. Who knows how many of the people who tour St. Simons Lighthouse do so in the hope of catching sight of the lighthouse keeper's ghost.

KENTUCKY

CAMPBELLSVILLE

Spurlington Train Tunnel

Work on the Spurlington Tunnel began on March 1, 1867. On average, it took a crew of seventy-five men twenty-four hours to bore through six feet of blue limestone. The thirty-one-mile rail line from Greensburg to Lebanon was completed on July 1, 1874. The first train went through the tunnel in October 1879. At one time, as many as four trains passed through the tunnel each day. Today, the Spurlington Train Tunnel is of interest primarily because of the legend of Nancy Bass.

Nancy Bass was rumored to be a witch who cursed people who crossed her. "Aunt Nancy," as she was known, was said to be a homeless wretch who spent the nights in haystacks and barns. To many people, she seemed to be a threat to the community. Some people even talked about burning her. Her untimely death gave rise to two tales that have been passed around Campbellsville, Kentucky, for generations. One legend has it that in a heated moment, she announced that she could be killed only by a silver bullet. One night, her lifeless body was discovered on the property of a man named Wright. Afterward, the coroner found a silver bullet embedded in her heart. In another version of the story, she was murdered after witnessing the James Gang bury their loot in the

Cumberland Mountains. People say that the gang buried her and the loot somewhere on top of the tunnel. Today, many locals claim to have captured the image of Nancy Bass when they photographed the entrance to the tunnel.

BEREA

Boone Tavern

Boone Tavern came into existence at the suggestion of Nellie Frost, the wife of Berea College president William G. Frost. In the early 1900s, Nellie argued, convincingly, that a new hotel was needed because of the increased enrollment at Berea College. In 1907, the New York architectural firm of Cady & See was hired to begin construction on the new hotel. Work on Boone Tavern was completed in 1909 at a cost of $20,000. Costs were kept down because college students fired the bricks at the campus brickyard. The College Woodworking Department was responsible for most of the construction.

Boone Tavern soon proved to be a good investment. During one summer, three hundred guests stayed at Boone Tavern. Over the years, a number of celebrities have stayed at the tavern, including Henry Ford, the Dalai Lama, Eleanor Roosevelt, President and Mrs. Coolidge, Robert Frost and Maya Angelou. Today, Boone Tavern is popular with visitors and ghost hunters alike.

In April 2012, a formal investigation of Boone Tavern was conducted by Ghost Chasers International. The group was drawn to Boone Tavern by stories told for years by employees about the voice of a little boy known only as "Timmy" that had been heard several times in the basement. Director Patti Starr and forty investigators spent a Friday and Saturday night at the old hotel. Afterward, Patti told Bill Robinson, a reporter for the *Richmond Register*, that "[Boone Tavern] is like a train station with spirits coming and going." Most of the paranormal activity took place in the basement and on the second floor. Using a device called a "spirit detector," the group was able to carry on a conversation with one of the resident spirits. Patti began by asking the spirits to say hello. Immediately, a faint "Hey" was heard over the spirit detector. When asked if he was "happy over there," a voice replied, "Quite a bit." Patti said that the investigators also made contact with the doctor who had tried, unsuccessfully, to save an injured little boy named Timmy in the hotel. He vowed to look in on Timmy "on the other side." Boone Tavern, it appears, is popular with both the living and the dead.

Louisville

The Dupont Mansion

Alfred Victor Dupont and his brother Biederman were two of the city's most successful businessmen in the second half of the nineteenth century. After arriving in Louisville in 1854, they founded A.V. Dupont and Company, which manufactured gunpowder and paper. In 1879, the Duponts built the Dupont Mansion at 1317 South Fourth Street in heart of the Old Louisville Historic District. The brothers had planned to use the magnificent three-story mansion as a "home away from home" for visiting relatives. The elegant ten-bedroom mansion has marble fireplaces, fourteen-foot ceilings, ten-foot doors and hardwood parquet floors. In 1886, the Duponts sold the mansion to Thomas Prather Jacob, the son of one of the wealthiest men in Louisville. Around the turn of the century, the Dupont Mansion was converted into an apartment house. By the 1990s, the once elegant mansion had fallen prey to the ravages of time and neglect. In the late 1990s, the old house was renovated and stabilized. In October 2000, Gayle and Herbert Warren bought the Dupont Mansion. One year later, the mansion was reopened as a bed-and-breakfast.

The Dupont Mansion is said to be haunted by the ghost of Alfred Victor Dupont, who led a secret life at the Galt Hotel. Alfred was a ladies' man who was rumored to have frequented bordellos. In 1893, his mistress told Alfred that she was pregnant with his baby. Alfred vehemently refused to take responsibility for the child, so his mistress shot him in the chest, killing him instantly. To avert a scandal, the Dupont family used its connections with the police and the newspaper to put a "spin" on Alfred's death. Until the truth came out in the 1930s, most of Louisville's citizens believed that Alfred died of a heart attack on the front porch of the Galt Hotel.

Alfred Victor Dupont is usually identified as the ghost that haunts the Dupont Mansion. Some speculate that because the Galt Hotel has been torn down, Alfred's spirit has taken up residence in the Dupont Mansion, which he visited on a regular basis. The most compelling reason for designating Alfred as the haunting spirit inside the old house is the ghost's apparent affinity for women. In his book *Phantoms of Old Louisville*, author David Domine tells the story of an interior decorator named Geraldine Beck who was walking down the stairwell between the third and second floors of the mansion when she felt someone blow in her ear. The next day, she was walking down the stairwell again. All of the sudden, an intensely cold feeling swept over her. Then she saw a man wearing a top hat and a nineteenth-century tuxedo walking down the stairs in front of her. He vanished when he reached the bottom of the stairs. The next day, Geraldine had an even closer encounter with the lustful ghost. She had just reached the bottom of the staircase when she felt someone's hand on her buttocks. She spun around, and no one was there. Suddenly, she felt someone grab her posterior again. She ran out of the room and, understandably, refrained from using the staircase during the rest of her time at the mansion.

The Octagon House

Determined to build a house that would stand out from the other plantation homes in Kentucky, Andrew Jackson Caldwell spent twelve years building his octagonal home. On February 13, 1862, the Confederate army camped out on the lawn of Jackson's home following its retreat from Bowling Green, the Confederate capital of Kentucky. Two days later, the Union army arrived at the Octagon House. The commanding officer suspected that the Caldwells had been hiding wounded Confederate soldiers in different places inside the house, so he decided to retaliate. The soldiers killed all of the cattle, including Mrs. Caldwell's favorite milking cow, Old Spot, and threw the dead animals into the well, polluting the water. The story goes that when the soldiers threatened to burn down the house, Caldwell responded, "Go right ahead. My brother just left, and he'll come back looking for you." Locals say that the Union army left the house intact, fearing the wrath of the angry old man.

The Caldwell family continued living in the Octagon House for several decades after Andrew Jackson Caldwell's death in 1866. In 1918, an osteopath from Nashville, Tennessee, Dr. Miles Williams, bought the house from Andrew's widow. Following his death in 1954, Dr. Williams's heirs turned the mansion into rental property. The historic home was acquired by the Octagon Hall Foundation in 2001, which is continuing its efforts to restore the only eight-sided house in Kentucky.

Billy Byrd, the curator of the Octagon House, is a virtual repository of the house's ghost stories, and he believes that the ghost of Andrew Jackson Caldwell may be the spectral figure that has been sighted riding a wagon in the back of the house. The ghost of a little girl who died in the fireplace in the basement kitchen in the 1860s has been credited with causing a fireplace kettle to swing on its movable arm during a Halloween tour in 2003. That same year, the unmistakable stench of rotting meat permeated the house. Later, a policeman who was responding to a burglar alarm inside the mansion was standing in the dark house with one of the restorers, getting his bearings, when he heard the jiggling of a doorknob. He pulled his gun and then made his way cautiously through the house. A few minutes later, the two men stared in disbelief as the knob on another door began to turn. Then the door opened on its own.

One of the most startling encounters inside the Octagon House occurred during a Civil War reenactment on the grounds of the plantation. A group of intrepid reenactors decided to spend the night inside the Octagon House, despite its haunted reputation. The sound of closing doors and spectral footsteps made sleeping inside the old house extremely difficult. The next morning, one of the men walked into an upstairs bedroom and was surprised to find the imprint of a body on the mattress because no one in his group had been sleeping there.

It seems as if the stubborn old man who defied the Union army will not permit even death to drive him from his beloved home.

LOUISIANA

LAFAYETTE

The Café Vermilionville

The Café Vermilionville is housed in what is reputed to be Lafayette's first inn. Constructed in 1799, the building is distinctive for its Anglo-American and French features. A Swiss immigrant named Henry Louis Monnier purchased the property in 1853. The inn was occupied by Union soldiers for a brief period during the Civil War. Legend has it that a jealous Frenchman shot and killed a Yankee captain who was paying too much attention to his wife. His son, Auguste Monnier, a prominent businessman, inherited the property after Henry's death. Auguste sold much of the Monnier property in 1875 but retained the two-story house. On May 30, 1882, a physician named M.E. Girard bought the old inn, which eventually became his retirement home. The property remained in the Girard family for several generations. M. Eloi Girard started a nursery on a portion of the property. Maurice Heymann bought the inn and the nursery from Merrick Girard in 1939. He eventually developed the nursery and the other landholdings of the Girard family into the Oil Center and Shopping Village. Heymann was planning to raze the historic inn, but he was prevented from doing so by Horace Rickey, who bought the old building. Rickey then set about renovating the old inn. He attached the kitchen, the dining room and the *garçonnière* to the old house, thereby creating 640 square feet of additional space. When the inn was transformed into the Café Vermilionville, the *garçonnière* was converted into the cocktail lounge. Two bars and a glass patio room were added on later. Today, when people order spirits with their meals, they might end up with the ethereal kind.

Most of the paranormal activity inside the old inn can be traced back to a tragic incident that occurred over 150 years ago when the inn was used as a private residence. A few years before the Civil War, the building was owned by a family with a little girl who was afflicted with polio. Her father, who lavished attention on the child, had to travel to New Orleans on a regular basis to buy his daughter the medicine that sustained her life. While her father was on one of these trips, the child died. The father, understandably, was wracked with guilt and remorse on his return.

The earliest recorded ghost stories date back to the time when the inn was being used as office space, just a few years before it was converted into the Café Vermilionville. A local woman who had driven by the building every morning between 4:00 a.m. and 5:00 a.m. stopped by one afternoon to tell one of the secretaries that she frequently saw a little girl in a yellow dress standing on the balcony. A few years later, after the Café Vermilionville opened up inside the old building, a man was standing in the restaurant, trying to photograph his wife before their meal was ready. He said when he looked through the viewfinder, he saw a little girl in a yellow dress, standing next to his wife. When he lowered the camera, the little spirit was gone.

In recent years, the little ghost has been seen many times in the Café Vermilionville. Apparently, all the changes that have been made to the structure have not made her feel unwelcome. For this little girl, the old inn will always be home, regardless of its appearance.

New Orleans

The Old U.S. Mint

The Old U.S. Mint, which has been declared a National Historic Landmark, is not only the oldest surviving building to have served as a U.S. Mint, but it is also the only structure in America to have served as both a U.S. Mint and as a Confederate Mint. Located on the northeastern edge of the French Quarter, the U.S. Mint was constructed in 1835 at the urging of President Andrew Jackson, who believed that a New Orleans mint would assist in the financial development of the western frontier. The Greek Revival building was designed by renowned architect William Strickland, one of the designers of the U.S. Capitol in Washington, D.C. Strickland went on to design the first four U.S. Mint buildings. A central Ionic portico makes up the north façade of the building. Inside the building, two large wings wrap around the central core to form a W-shaped structure. Because Strickland did not account for New Orleans' high water table, the New Orleans Mint had to be reinforced with iron rods in 1840. In 1854, Pierre Gustave Toutant Beauregard fireproofed the mint and rebuilt the basement arches. After the mint minted its first thirty dimes on March 8, 1838, it proceeded to strike many different denominations of either silver or gold.

The New Orleans Mint's first tour of duty extended from 1838 to January 26, 1861, when Louisiana seceded from the United States. The Federal employees who had been working at the mint were permitted to keep their jobs as employees of Louisiana. In 1861, the New Orleans Mint struck 962,633 half dollars, a large number of which had alternate reverse dies. After the New Orleans Mint ran out of bullion on April 1, 1861, Confederate troops were quartered in the building until the city was taken by Admiral David G. Farragut's naval forces.

The mint building was closed until 1876, when it reopened as an assay office. The building's second tour of duty as a U.S. Mint began in 1879, when the superintendent of the U.S. Mint, Dr. M.F. Bonzano, recommended that the old mint be refurbished. After new minting equipment was installed, the New Orleans Mint produced silver coins, including the Morgan silver dollar, from 1879 to 1904. Women were hired during this time to weigh the unstamped coin planchets and to serve as counters and packers and to work at the coining presses. The New Orleans Mint was closed in 1909 because the main mint at Philadelphia was effectively meeting the need for coinage in the United States.

The old U.S. Mint Building in New Orleans served a variety of purposes over the next seven decades. Between 1909 and 1932, the building was again converted into an assay office. A federal prison was housed there between 1932 and 1943, when the U.S. Coast Guard used it as a storage facility. By 1966, the Old U.S. Mint Building had stood abandoned for many years and had fallen into decay. The State of Louisiana agreed to save the structure from the wrecking ball on the condition that it would be renovated within fifteen years. In 1981, the Old U.S. Mint opened as part of the Louisiana State Museum complex.

The museum had not been open for very long before rumors began circulating about ghosts inside the old building. Employees have been touched and lights flicker. Motion-activated alarms occasionally go off for seemingly no reason. The door in one of the museum's storerooms has been known to open and close on its own. Employees have seen an apparition, and a shadowy figure has been spotted on the first floor. Thuds, bumps and other noises have also been heard on the first floor.

One of the employees who has seen the ghost on the first floor is the curator, Sarah Elizabeth Gundlach. Late one afternoon, she left the main entry desk and was getting ready to close up. She was on her way downstairs when she noticed a dramatic drop in temperature. She then caught a glimpse of a head and shoulders floating above the floor. She did a double take and looked away for an instant. When she turned back around, the apparition was gone.

Other employees have also had strange experiences inside the museum. Security guard Jimmy Jackson saw a male apparition on the second floor five times. Jackson concluded that the figure was a male because it had a beard. The first time he saw the ghost, the specter was standing against a wall at the end of a row of jail cells. The apparition was wearing ragged clothing. Jackson distinctly recalled that it had black hair. Other employees who have seen the ghost describe him as a male dressed in prison stripes. He is often seen standing around smoking. Because no one knows the name of the ghost, the employees have dubbed him "Lonesome Larry."

Several of the Old U.S. Mint's other ghosts have been identified. One of the ghosts is said to be the spirit of a steamboat gambler named William Mumford. In April 1862, he climbed to the roof of the mint and tore down the U.S. flag the U.S. Marines had raised the same day. Mumford ripped the flag into shreds and stuffed them into his shirt. Mumford was captured the next day. The military governor of New Orleans, Union general Benjamin Franklin Butler, ordered his execution. On June 7, 1862, Mumford was hanged from a flagstaff that projected horizontally from the mint. His ghost is affectionately called "Poor Mumford." The female ghost that has been seen throughout the building is said to be the spirit of William Mumford's mother, who was heartbroken at the loss of her son. The weeping that occasionally echoes through the building is usually attributed to Mrs. Mumford. The ghost of an employee who was crushed in one of the coin presses could also be haunting the building.

An investigation of the haunted museum was conducted by the Atlantic Paranormal Society (TAPS) in 2010. During the investigation, the group heard a series of shuffles, pings, bumps and clicks. One of the investigators, K.J., saw what he thought was a shadow figure. Two other investigators, Steve Gonsalves and Dave Tango, were walking through the second floor when the balcony door in front of them opened and slammed shut on its own. The pair was unable to debunk the phenomenon. Despite the investigators' personal experiences, the group did not collect enough physical evidence to declare the Old U.S. Mint haunted.

Even though TAPS did not film any full-bodied apparitions or collect any compelling EVPs, the Old U.S. Mint still has the reputation for being the most haunted museum in the entire city. Granted, many people visit the museum to view permanent exhibits like the New Orleans Jazz exhibit, the Mississippi and the Making of a Nation exhibit or the Newcomb Pottery and Crafts exhibit. However, the popularity of the Old U.S. Mint's ghost stories has to be at least partially responsible for the large number of tourists who visit the historic structure each year.

The Sausage Maker's Ghost

In the 1920s, a German immigrant named Hans Mueller operated a butcher's shop inside the old house at 725 Ursuline Street. Hans and his wife, Teresa, had arrived in America from Germany at the turn of the century. Their specialty was sausage, which they made with a mixture of Cajun and Creole spices. Not long after the Muellers opened their business, word spread that they had the best sausage in town. People came from miles around to sample the Muellers' unique blend of German and Creole sausage. As the money poured in, the Muellers were certain that they had made the right decision in moving to New Orleans.

Unfortunately, the Muellers' happiness was short-lived. Two legends have been generated by the residents of New Orleans to explain their downfall. One legend has it that people flocked to the Muellers' butcher shop for more than just the sausage. Hans Mueller was reputed to be a charismatic individual who was especially attractive to women. As time passed, Hans began paying less attention to his wife, who had become fat, and more attention to a German girl he had just hired to help out in the shop. The girl, whose name was Ilse, was just as attractive as Teresa had been before the years of drinking beer and eating sausage had added pounds to her once-svelte figure. Before long, Ilse became his mistress. Hans and his comely employee conducted their clandestine affair after hours when his wife was asleep.

According to another version of the legend, Teresa was responsible for the demise of their marriage. Some people say that she loved alcohol and strange men much more than she loved her husband, for whom making money had become the most important thing in life. She began frequenting the local bars and bedding down with men while her husband was gone. Not only did her housekeeping suffer as a result of her nightly excursions, but so did the couple's three small children, who roamed around the house unclothed and unfed.

No one living today knows for sure what precipitated the horrible events that transpired on October 28, 1927. Some say that Hans buried a meat cleaver in Teresa's brain one night when she accused him of cheating on her with Ilse. Others believe that he bashed her in the head when she returned from one of her nightly rendezvous. Another variant of the tale holds that Hans crept behind Teresa one night, wrapped a piece of rope around her neck and choked her to death. After he regained his composure, Hans was faced with the problem of disposing of his wife's mutilated body. He looked around the room, and his eyes settled on the huge sausage grinder, which turned pork and beef into the spicy delicacies that had become favorites of New Orleans. Hans picked up Teresa's lifeless body and dumped it into the sausage grinder. He fully intended to convert Teresa into one hundred kilos of sausage.

For a short while, Hans conducted business as usual. When his neighbors asked him about his wife, he simply said that she was out of town visiting neighbors or that she was upstairs in bed, recovering from an illness. He decided to keep his relationship with Ilse a secret to avoid arousing suspicion in the neighborhood.

Hans's crime did not stay hidden for very long. The guilt that was tearing him apart began to affect his appearance. The formerly clean-cut butcher was disheveled. His eyes were bloodshot from lack of sleep, and his hair was shaggy and uncombed. Even worse, customers began complaining about finding bits of bone and pieces of cloth in their sausage. One morning, a customer was eating the sausage when she bit down on a gold wedding ring. After vomiting what she had already eaten, she called the police, who raided the Muellers' butcher shop. They found the proprietor huddled in the corner, shaking and crying uncontrollably. After he calmed down, he explained that the night before, he had heard a thumping noise coming from the back of the shop. When he walked over to the sausage grinder, Hans was shocked to see his wife's corpse climbing out of the vat. Her head and face were horribly mutilated. Teresa staggered toward her husband with arms outstretched. After a few seconds, Teresa's ghastly appearance and blood-curdling moans proved to be too much for the man. He ran out into the street screaming. When his neighbors asked him what had happened, Hans explained that he had had a bad dream. By the time the police arrived the next morning, Hans had not totally recovered from his wife's unwelcome return. He told the police that his dead wife was trying to kill him. Hans was committed to an insane asylum.

Mueller's sausage business was taken over by another man. The new owner had great difficulty keeping employees because of the frequent sightings of Teresa Mueller's ghost, who stumbled around the back room, looking for her husband. The sightings ceased altogether after Hans Mueller suffered a complete mental breakdown and committed suicide.

The murder of Hans Mueller's wife, Teresa, has become known as one of the most lurid crimes in New Orleans, a city that is renowned for its sensationalistic murders. Hans's story lives on in the ghost stories that people still tell about his butcher shop; in the 1974 movie *The Mad Butcher*, starring actor Victor Buono; and in the family stories of New Orleans residents whose ancestors discovered an unexpected "bonus" inside their breakfast sausage.

The Griffin House

The Griffin House at 1447 Constance Street was built in 1852 by Adam Griffin, who abandoned the house only a few months after the occupation of Union troops under the command of General Benjamin Butler began in the spring of 1862. General Butler commandeered the Griffin House for use as a barracks and as a storage house for supplies. When the soldiers climbed the stairs to the attic, they were greeted with a sight that rivaled any of the horrors on the battlefield. Several slaves in various states of starvation were chained to the walls. Some of the slaves had maggot-infested wounds on their arms, legs and faces. This was not the only horror to take place in the house. In his book *Gumbo Ya-Ya*, Lyle Saxon tells the story of two Union soldiers who were arrested for stealing army funds. The two men were held prisoner on the third floor of the Griffin House while awaiting trial. In another version of the legend, the two Union soldiers were actually

Confederate deserters who were wearing uniforms at the time of the robbery. Somehow, the prisoners got their hands on two bottles of cheap whiskey and proceeded to get roaring drunk. For the next few hours, the men sang "John Brown's Body" as loudly as they could. Some local historians believe that the two men sang this particular song, which was very popular with Union soldiers, to convince their captors that they actually were Yankees, not Confederates. When they finished singing, the prisoners bribed one of the guards to give each of them a pistol. The men lay in bed, facing each other, and on the count of three, each man fired a bullet into the other man's heart. Repercussions from this double suicide have resonated from the Griffin House for many years in the form of ghost stories.

After the Civil War, the Griffin House was home to a number of businesses. For a while, it was used as a mattress factory and a perfume bottling plant. In the 1920s, the Griffin House was leased by a man who rebuilt air conditioners. The man told his customers and neighbors that he had "seen things" in the house. One day, the man failed to show up for work. He was never heard from again.

In the 1930s, the Griffin House was converted into a lamp factory. According to Lyle Saxon, a black janitor was staying late to clean up the lamp factory in 1936. He was working on the second floor when a door opened on its own. He then heard what sounded like a pair of heavy boots walking out of the room, right toward him. The sound was so loud that it was almost deafening. A few minutes later, the janitor heard another pair of boots walk by, following by the sound of someone whistling "John Brown's Body." The janitor threw down his broom and ran out of the house.

Not long thereafter, the owner of the lamp factory, Isadore Seeling, had just entered the building one morning with his brother when a huge block of cement came hurtling down the stairs, right at them. Isadore barely avoided death when his brother pushed him out of the way. Neither of the men had seen the cement block before. They ran upstairs to find out who had tried to kill them. There was no one there. Adding to the mystery, the floor had been painted the day before and was still tacky, yet no footprints could be found in the paint. In addition, all of the doors and windows were locked.

A few years later, the old building became a boardinghouse. One day, a widow was sitting in a chair by a window in her room on the second floor. Her knitting was interrupted by what appeared to be spot of blood on her hand. She wiped off the blood, thinking that she must have scratched herself. When a second spot of blood appeared, the widow looked up and was shocked to see blood oozing from a crack in the ceiling. She ran out of the room, screaming. The widow refused to return to the boardinghouse, and her relatives stopped by to retrieve her possessions. They looked up at the ceiling and saw no trace of blood in any of the cracks. However, as they locked the front door, they saw two young men in Union army uniforms looking down at them from a second-story window.

In the 1940s, a policeman named William Fleming told Lyle Saxon that when he was a child, he and two other boys entered the Griffin House with a couple of dogs. They entered an upstairs room where the floor had been torn up and entertained themselves by walking on the joists. Suddenly, the door slowly opened, and an icy blast of wind filled the room. One of the dogs fell through the hole in the floor and was killed instantly. The other dog whined and jumped around. The boys decided that playtime was over, and they ran out of the room. As they were leaving the house, they heard phantom voices singing "John Brown's Body."

In August 1951, a devastating hurricane struck New Orleans. The pounding wind and waves of water completely destroyed the slave quarters behind the Griffin House. Workers digging through the debris uncovered a tunnel that ran under the house and led out into the street. They also discovered several old uniforms and a large chest inside the tunnel.

In the late 1970s, Kathleen and Anthony Jones purchased the Griffin House. They told Richard Winer and Nancy Osborn, authors of the book *Haunted Houses*, that they had not experienced anything out of the ordinary since they moved into the old mansion. However, a black man who lived across the street told them that at ten o'clock one night, he walked out to his driveway and discovered that one of his tires was flat. While he was changing the tire, he heard loud, maniacal laughter coming from the Griffin House. A few seconds later, he heard the sound of smashing glass. The man knew that something was not right because the Griffin House had been abandoned for a long time.

By the 1980s, the Griffin House was abandoned once again. Like many old, empty houses in the neighborhood, the Griffin House was taken over by drug addicts. After a month, though, not even the drug addicts could stay in the house for very long. One of the drug addicts said that he saw two men in blue uniforms—like police uniforms—and they were singing "old-timey" songs. Today, the Griffin House has been completely restored and is a private residence. So far, the owners have not encountered the phantom soldiers or anything else unusual inside the house.

The Ghost of the French Quarter Opera House

In the nineteenth century, New Orleans was, to use a modern term, one of the most diverse cities in the United States. French, Spanish, Italian and African American communities coexisted in relative harmony. The taboos against intermarriage between different ethnic and racial groups were not nearly as strong in New Orleans as in other parts of the United States. One of the products of one of these marriages was Marguerite O'Donnell, the daughter of a French mother and an Irish father. To escape the grinding poverty that she and her twelve siblings had been born into, Marguerite married Octave Sauve in 1860, when she was eighteen years old. Octave was an absinthe addict who forced Marguerite to cook and clean and to submit to frequent beatings. She was convinced that her beauty entitled her to a more refined life than that of a scullery maid.

Marguerite's life changed forever in 1875 when she found a place on the chorus line at the French Quarter Opera House. Even though she was in her early thirties, she still retained enough of her youthful beauty to attract the attention of a number of young men, who became her lovers. After all of her siblings and her husband, Octave, perished in the yellow fever epidemic of 1878, she became the mistress of a wealthy, elderly gentleman named Monsieur de Boisblan, who showered the former chorus girl with gifts. He was so attracted to her that he left her $10,000 after his death.

Knowing that she probably would not be able to depend on the kindness of wealthy benefactors anymore, Marguerite invested her inheritance in Les Camillias, a confectionary shop in the French Quarter. Before long, people from all walks of life frequented Les Camillias. She hired four pastry chefs between 1878 and 1880, all of whom tried to convince her that she needed a husband. Knowing that the young men were only interested in her money, she rebuked all of their advances. Between 1878 and 1880, she embarked on a torrid affair with an indigo merchant named Silas McIver. Marguerite broke off the relationship after finding out that he was cheating on her with a young girl named Colette de Bourgon.

Marguerite had resigned herself to being one of those poor souls who are unlucky in love when Carlos Alfara entered her life. Carlos was a handsome twenty-one-year-old who answered Marguerite's want ad in the local newspaper for a pastry chef. Even though Carlos knew very little about pastry, he was skilled in the art of love. Marguerite and Carlos almost immediately became lovers. She lavished him with a complete set of clothes and other expensive gifts.

The French Quarter Opera House. *Courtesy of the Library of Congress.*

Marguerite's romantic bliss with the man of her dreams came to an abrupt end one night when her young lover, mumbling in the throes of an alcohol-induced stupor, referred to her as Lisette, a drug-addicted prostitute who frequented the Old Absinthe House. She became even more incensed when she realized that Carlos had probably given the fallen woman some of the gifts and money that Marguerite had given him.

Convinced that life was not worth living without true love, the despondent woman cut Carlos out of her will and scribbled a suicide note on a piece of stationery. She then walked down to the opera house, where she hid the suicide note in the rafters above the stage. Marguerite trudged back home, put a loaded pistol to her head and pulled the trigger.

Some people say that Marguerite's anger was not fully snuffed out by the bullet that passed through her skull. Three days after her funeral, a witness walking through the French Quarter at midnight claimed to have seen a translucent apparition that bore an uncanny resemblance to Marguerite leave the opera house, glide down Bourbon Street and make its way to an apartment building on the corner of Dumaine and Royal Streets, where Carlos and Lisette lay sleeping. The next morning, the other tenants notified the fire department that the pungent smell of gas was coming from Carlos and Lisette's apartment. When the firemen broke down the door, they discovered the bodies of the illicit lovers lying in bed.

The coroner certified their death as a suicide. However, people living in the neighborhood were convinced that Marguerite's spirit had taken her revenge on her unfaithful lover and his girlfriend. For many years, her ghost has been sighted walking down Toulouse Street and the Rue Royale. Marguerite's frightful-looking apparition has also been seen walking around the building on the corner of Dumaine and Royal, which today is known as the Naighi Building. Witnesses describe Marguerite as having long, white hair that trails behind her on her lonely walks through the French Quarter in a tattered, white shroud. Her eyes are bloodshot, and tears stream down her face. One of the most compelling tales of Marguerite's spirit is told by Victor C. Klein, author of *New Orleans Ghosts II*. On December 4, 1919, the same day that a tenant living in Marguerite's old apartment burned a letter written by Marguerite, the French Quarter Opera House was completely destroyed by fire.

Woodland Plantation

In 1790, William Johnson and his partner, Captain George Brandish, emigrated from Nova Scotia to southeast Louisiana, where Johnson became the country's first chief river pilot. Johnson also became a highly successful sugar planter. However, Johnson's fame was tarnished when he entered into the slave trade with Bradish and the notorious pirate Jean Lafitte. In 1793, Johnson and Brandish built Magnolia Plantation. The two men lived there with their families until 1834, when Johnson and his four sons built Woodland Plantation four miles away. Eventually, Johnson's eldest son, Brandish, inherited the plantation, and he continued to own it until his death in 1897. The Wilkinson family bought the plantation from Brandish's heirs and owned it until 1997.

Woodland Plantation's beauty and reputation suffered a steep decline in the twentieth century. Bootleggers traveling down the Mississippi used the plantation as a convenient drop-off point for their liquor during Prohibition. By the 1940s, Woodland Plantation was a dilapidated wreck, overgrown with trees and bushes. In 1965, Hurricane Betsy completely destroyed the four brick slave cabins and inflicted considerable damage to the plantation house. For the next three decades, Woodland Plantation stood neglected and abandoned, a pale, tragic shadow of its former self.

The fine old mansion was rescued from sheer obliteration by Claire and Jacques Creppel and their son, Foster, who bought Woodland Plantation at auction in 1997. At the time they acquired the old building, it was missing most of its doors and windows and was inhabited by owls, pigeons, rats and alligators.

The Creppels immediately began to suspect that they had acquired more than just an old house when they started restoring it. In his book *Ghost Hunter's Guide to New Orleans*, author Jeff Dwyer tells the story of Foster Creppel's first three months inside the house while he and his parents were restoring. Foster said that he slept in the house all by himself most of the time. On many occasions, he was awakened by the sound of footsteps on the second floor of the house. He also heard a distinct tapping sound. Foster likened the sound to the tapping of a cane on the wooden floors. After experiencing a number of sleepless nights in the house, Foster proclaimed his intention of burning down the house if the ghosts woke him up again.

Other spirit activity has been reported in the old house over the years. The ghost of Brandish Johnson has been seen wearing striped pants and a top hat. Most of the witnesses describe him as carrying a gold-tipped cane. The ghost of a little boy has appeared in one of the bedrooms. He usually disappears when the occupant of the room asks him questions, such as "Who are you?" or "What are you doing here?" The ghosts of a man accompanied by two women have been spotted on the first floor. The ghosts of slaves who were chained to the walls of the four brick slave quarters are now said to haunt Spirit Hall, a reconstructed Catholic church that was moved to this site in 1999. Paranormal investigators who have visited Woodland Plantation believe that the old mansion is haunted, either because the eternal rest of the spirits has been disturbed by the alterations made in the house or because they feel much more comfortable in the mansion now that its former glory has been restored.

Arnaud's

Most residents of New Orleans think of Arnaud's Restaurant primarily as one of the city's finest eateries. The restaurant was founded in 1920 by a colorful wine merchant named Arnaud Cazenave. Unlike at most restaurants in the city, Arnaud's master chef was a woman named Madame Pierre. Cazenave was known locally as "Count" Arnaud, despite the fact that no noble blood ran through his veins. Following Arnaud's death, his daughter, Germaine Cazenave Wells, took over the restaurant. In the 1970s, she leased the New Orleans landmark to outside owners.

Even though Arnaud's is no longer owned by the Cazenave family, the original owner's authoritative presence is still very evident. Count Arnaud, who believed that a New Orleans restaurant should serve its customers in the grand French style, had strict rules regarding table settings. Today, waiters and waitresses claim that if silverware and napkins are not properly arranged at closing time, the next morning, the table setting will be rearranged in a manner that Count Arnaud would have approved of.

In 1983, then-owner Archie A. Casbarian opened up the Germaine Cazenave Wells Mardi Gras Museum inside the restaurant. The museum features a lavish assortment of costumes worn during Mardi Gras and thirteen of Germaine Cazenave Wells's queen costumes. Costumes worn by Germaine's mother and daughter and four king costumes worn by Count Arnaud are also on display. On several occasions, sightings of the shadowy form of Germaine Cazenave Wells have been reported.

Many employees believe that the scariest part of the old restaurant is the wine cellar. According to Victor C. Klein, author of *New Orleans Ghosts III*, employees who have been down in the wine cellar all alone have been startled by the sound of labored breathing, as if someone is standing behind them. A few employees claim that they have been touched by an invisible hand.

Staff at the restaurant believe that two ghosts are haunting Arnaud's. One of these ghosts is said to be the spirit of Germaine Cazenave Wells. Her ghost has been seen floating out of the ladies' restroom. Witnesses describe her as wearing an evening gown and a big hat. However, the most commonly sighted apparition inside the restaurant is the ghost of the count himself. In his book *Ghost Hunter's Guide to New Orleans*, author Jeff Dwyer says that Arnaud's ghost has been seen dressed in his trademark tuxedo, walking through the bars, kitchen and dining areas. The count's ghost usually appears when a waiter or waitress accidentally spills a drink or drops a tray or silverware.

Arnaud's is famous for such Creole dishes as Shrimp Arnaud and red fish filet, basted in the count's own spicy recipe for remoulade sauce. Guests are also treated to a taste of Old World elegance in the restaurant's luxurious dining rooms and in the French 75 Bar. Only fairly recently has the fine old restaurant become renowned for its ghostly activity.

Bayou Grand Caillou

Legends about buried pirate treasure can be found in the lore of most of the Gulf States. Most of these stories focus on the ill-gotten gains of Jean Lafitte and Blackbeard. Louisiana's most famous lost treasure story takes place in Bayou Grand Caillou in southern Louisiana.

Many variants of the following story exist, but the best-known variant was collected by Lyle Saxon for his book *Gumbo Ya-Ya*. Years ago, a quadroon fisherman named Louis lived and worked on Bayou Grand Caillou. Although Louis did not hate his occupation, he longed to find an easier way to make his money. One day, Louis decided to investigate stories he had heard about buried pirate treasure on a muddy little island called L'Isle de Gombi. The island was named after Gombi, a buccaneer who had fought alongside Jean Lafitte. His friends tried to talk Louis out of going, but they said that if he must go, the best time to search for treasure would be at night during a full moon. The burial spot of the treasure was supposedly marked by a small grassy spot that glowed in the moonlight.

After he had summoned up enough courage, Louis loaded his pirogue with a shovel, lantern and other supplies. He made it to the nearby island in less than an hour. Louis pulled his pirogue ashore and, with the wind howling around his head, began to dig. He had not been digging for very long before he noticed that somehow, his small boat had made its way back into the water. Louis hurried over to his boat before it floated it away. He tied it up securely and resumed digging.

While Louis was digging, he was overcome by the creepy feeling that he was being watched. Louis lifted up his weary head and noticed two pairs of hairy, brown feet standing on the edge of his hole. Louis gasped and backed away from the two intruders, who were dressed like pirates from the eighteenth century. The ghastly figures appeared to be totally waterlogged. Tiny sea creature scuttled out of their beards and clothing. Seaweed dripped from their arms and legs. Each man clutched a rusty cutlass in his bony hand. As the soggy pirates staggered in his direction with menacing looks on their faces, Louis fell to his knees, closed his eyes and prayed to the Blessed Virgin, vowing never to look for treasure again if she delivered him safely from the pirates. After reciting his prayer for the seventh time, Louis slowly opened his eyes. The pirates were gone.

Breathing a sigh of relief, Louis ran back down the beach. When his little boat came into sight, he stopped dead in his tracks because sitting in the pirogue was a third pirate, a very large man with a big belly. He wore a long coat and a big, brass belt buckle. Clots of blood and tiny shrimp dripped from his bushy black beard. He held a large pistol that, in Louis's fevered imagination, seemed as big as a cannon. A voice that appeared to come from a blacksmith's bellows ordered Louis to row. The terrified fisherman dropped his shovel and lantern and jumped in the pirogue. Louis proceeded to row as fast as he could away from Gombi Island.

When the pirogue was a few leagues away from the island, the pirate stuffed his pistol into his belt and fell over backwards into the ocean. Louis was certain that he had been in the presence of the ghost of the pirate Gombi because no bubbles came to the surface of the water. By the time Louis made it back home, he was in a daze. He stumbled into his house and opened the door to his bedroom. His appearance was so altered by his terrifying encounter that his wife almost shot him when he entered the bedroom. His hair was as white as snow, and his eyes seemed to be focused on something very far away. In one version of the tale, Louis climbed into bed and died sometime during the night. Another variant has it that Louis never smiled or talked very much after returning from Gombi Island. He related the tale of his meeting with the ghostly pirates to anyone who would listen. Louis's friends, who were convinced that his story was true, were amazed that he was still sane after returning home. After a few months, Louis died in his sleep.

Hotel St. Pierre

The Hotel St. Pierre at 919 Burgundy Street is composed of eleven small Creole cottages, some of which were used as slave quarters. One of these buildings was constructed by Gabriel Peyroux de la Roche in 1780. A native of France, Peyroux originally built his house on a plantation on Bayou Road. Peyroux later moved the house to its present location on Burgundy Street, where his wife's father once owned property. The Peyroux family owned the house until 1850, and the old house is now the main office of the Hotel St Pierre. The other cottages were added on between 1916 and 1950 by D.H. Holmes, Ltd., to create a department store.

The Hotel St. Pierre is said to be haunted by the ghost of Peyroux's carriage master. In his book *Ghost Hunter's Guide to New Orleans*, author Jeff Dwyer says that the apparition has been sighted on the carriageway at all hours of the day. Witnesses describe the ghost as a black man wearing a blue shirt, blue pants and shiny black boots. The apparition appears to be in his mid-forties. The carriage master's ghost seems to be dutifully awaiting the carriages that pulled in and out of the carriageway.

In September 1996, Dr. Larry Montz, the director of the International Society for Paranormal Research (ISPR) investigative team, visited the Hotel St. Pierre in response to a request by the director. The team detected the presence not only of the carriage master but of a Confederate soldier as well. Guests have reported seeing the shadowy figure of a man in a gray uniform.

San Francisco Plantation

In 1827, Elisee Rillieux, a free man of color, began creating a huge plantation by buying up large tracts of land. In 1830, Edmond Bozonier Marmillion and his partner, Eugene Lartigue, paid $100,000 for the plantation, where Edmond had planned to plant sugar cane. Edmond and his wife, Antoinette, had eight children, six of whom died of tuberculosis. Antoinette succumbed to the disease in 1843. Edmond began construction of an eleven-thousand-square-foot plantation house in 1853 with the intention of leaving it to his two surviving sons, Charles and Vaslin. Artisans fashioned the exquisite faux marbling, painted door panels, painted ceilings and faux wood graining throughout the mansion. From the river, the plantation house was said to resemble a steamboat.

Edmond died in 1856, not long after he had finished the construction of his mansion, which he named Marmillion. Charles and Vaslin tried to sell the estate in 1859, but the sale was opposed by their sister-in-law, Zoe Luminais. In 1861, Charles was pressed into service in the Confederate army. He was promoted to the rank of captain and fought in four major battles, including Gettysburg. Charles was captured by the Union army, but he escaped not long thereafter. He was captured a second time and remained a prisoner for two years. By the time he was released, his legs were severely injured.

After the war, Charles returned to Marmillion Plantation. He was joined by his brother Vaslin and his wife, Louise. She spent so much money furnishing the huge house that Vaslin renamed the plantation *Fruschin*, which means "without a penny in my pocket." Within a few years, Charles and Vaslin made a fortune on their sugar cane crop, even though Vaslin never really fancied himself a sugar cane planter.

In 1878, the plantation was purchased by Achille D. Bougere for $50,000. He changed the name of the plantation to San Francisco. However, the plantation was not nearly as productive under Bougere's ownership. When he died in 1887, he had serious financial problems. Bourgere's wife and sons tried to run the plantation on their own for almost two decades. After selling the plantation to Schmidt and Ziegler for $80,000, they moved to New Orleans. Five years later, the plantation passed into the hands of the Ory family, who set up the San Francisco Planting & Manufacturing Company. During their fifty-year stay in the house, the Ory family modernized the old house by adding bathrooms and a kitchen, but the remainder of the antebellum mansion remained unaltered.

A new levee was constructed by the Army Corps of Engineers between 1927 and 1932. Lobbying efforts by local residents persuaded the Louisiana legislature to pass a bill that saved San Francisco Plantation by curving the levee around it. In 1954, Mr. and Mrs. Thompson leased the old plantation from the Ory family and immediately set about preserving it so that it could serve as a tour home. After Mr. Thompson died, his widow moved out, and the house was bought first by the ECOL Company and then by Marathon Oil. Thousands of dollars were spent restoring the house to the way it would have looked just before the Civil War. Today, over 100,000 people visit San Francisco Plantation each year, not just because it is an atypical antebellum home but also because it is reputed to be haunted.

San Francisco Plantation is said to be haunted by several ghosts. Charles Marmillion's apparition has been seen in the main-floor office, the dining room and one of the bedrooms. Witnesses describe him as wearing a long coat. His spirit has also been sighted smoking a cigar as he walks through the grounds. The ghosts of Vaslin and Louise's daughters have also been seen playing together under the trees. The girls are usually wearing white dresses.

In the late 1990s, a formal investigation of San Francisco Plantation was conducted by the ISPR investigative team. Members of the team follow a strict policy of going into a site completely ignorant of its history or its paranormal occurrences. During the night, one of the clairvoyants who assisted the team sensed the presence of a man in his mid-thirties who was lying in a first-floor bedroom. The clairvoyant identified him as "Charles." The former owner's spirit was also detected in an office on the ground floor by two other clairvoyants on the team. They described him as a man with a red beard and moustache. He wore a brown coat. On the second floor, other team members encountered the ghosts of two little girls, one of whom was very sick. The Marmillion family, it seems, is having great difficulty relinquishing ownership of San Francisco Plantation, even after death.

Napoleon House Restaurant

Located at 500 Chartres Street in New Orleans, Napoleon House was built in 1814 for Nicholas Girod, who served as mayor of New Orleans from 1814 to 1815. According to local legend, Girod announced during a party held at this mansion in 1821 that Napoleon was welcome to live at his fine house in New Orleans if he ever escaped from Elba Island. Girod made the offer, knowing full well that Napoleon's chances of escaping were slim to none. However, Girod's display of generosity garnered him considerable public support during his lifetime. Ever since, the old building has been known locally as "Napoleon House." During the Civil War, the second floor of Napoleon House was used as a hospital for Union and Confederate soldiers. A number of different families lived in Napoleon House during the second half of the nineteenth century. Since 1914, Napoleon House has been owned and operated as a restaurant by the Impastato family. A portrait of Pete Impastato, who owned the restaurant from 1936 to 1971, hangs inside

The ghost of a Civil War soldier has been seen on the balcony of the Napoleon House. *Courtesy of the author.*

the restaurant. Ironically, the ghosts that haunt the old building are probably not the spirits of the Impastatos or any of the other families who have owned the structure down through the years.

Napoleon House is haunted by the spirits of people who perished there in the nineteenth century. The apparition of a man in a gray uniform who is seen on the balcony facing Chartres Street is probably the ghost of one of the Civil War soldiers who succumbed to his wounds there. The restaurant is also haunted by the spirit of a black woman, most likely a governess or "mammy," who wears a long skirt and a headscarf. Because she is usually sighted in the courtyard, many people believe that she died there. Jeff Dwyer, author of *Ghost Hunter's Guide to New Orleans*, reports that "Mammy's" spirit was particularly active during the 1990s when the old building was being renovated. Her mischievous spirit was blamed for much of the poltergeist-like activity that took place in the bar, such as the spilling of drinks. "Mammy's" ghost seemed to have settled down after the renovations were completed.

Today, customers come to Napoleon House for the opportunity to bask in its Old World grandeur. Guests can listen to Beethoven's "Eroica," composed in praise of Napoleon, while drinking a Pimm's Cup.

Saint Louis Cemetery No. 1

New Orleans is unlike any other place in the United States. The old city's distinctive food, architecture and customs attract thousands of tourists every year. Even the cemeteries in New Orleans seem to belong to another time and place. One of the city's most unusual—and haunted—cemeteries is Saint Louis Cemetery No. 1.

Saint Louis Cemetery No. 1 is the oldest cemetery in New Orleans. Founded in 1789, it is located at the corner of St. Louis Street and Basin Street. The encroachment of modern development in the city has claimed much of the cemetery's original acreage. Even though the cemetery covers only one square block, over 100,000 bodies are buried there. Some of the people who are spending their eternal rest in Saint Louis Cemetery No. 1 are Etienne de Bore, the first mayor of New Orleans; Homer Plessy, the plaintiff from the 1896 *Plessy v. Ferguson* Supreme Court case; Barthelemy Lafon, an architect who became one of Jean Lafitte's pirates; Paul Morphy, one of the world's first chess champions; and Marie Laveau, known as the "Voodoo Queen of New Orleans." The old cemetery achieved even wider fame when it was used as a location setting in the films *Easy Rider* and *Interview with a Vampire*.

Many visitors to St. Louis Cemetery No. 1 have marked *X*'s on Marie Laveau's tomb for good luck. *Courtesy of the author.*

Because the city is below sea level, most of the dead are interred in mausoleums and vaults. Corpses are laid in wooden coffins and placed inside the tombs for one year and a day. During this period, the heat inside the vaults is so intense that most of the bodies are reduced to ashes, earning the tombs the colorful name "ovens." At the end of the waiting period, the remains are placed in bags, which are moved to the rear of the tomb to create space for more bodies.

Saint Louis Cemetery has been in constant use since the first bodies were interred in 1789. The cemetery was listed on the National Register of Historic Places in 1975. In 2004, many of the old tombs were restored. Today, the cemetery is owned and operated by the Archdiocese of New Orleans.

Naturally, the oldest cemetery in New Orleans is populated with the ghosts of the occupants of the tombs and vaults, as well as with their earthly remains. One of these restless spirits is the ghost of a man named Henry Vignes. Witnesses describe him as a tall man wearing a white shirt who taps people on the shoulder and asks them the location of his vault. The spirit of Henry Vignes is a classic example of a "lost soul" who is doomed to carry on his eternal search for a final resting place.

The cemetery's most famous ghost is undoubtedly the spirit of Marie Laveau. Her tomb is noteworthy for the *X*'s visitors have scratched on the side for good luck. Devotees of the Voodoo Queen of New Orleans have also left behind tokens, such as jewelry, candles, bones, flowers and money. The ghost of Marie Laveau is said to be an unhappy spirit who walks around her tomb chanting curses. Some people claim that the unhappy specter even slapped a man who was examining her tomb. People have also seen a host of nude phantoms performing a voodoo ritual around her tomb. A few people have walked through cold spots and have felt the icy touch of dead fingers in the vicinity of Marie Laveau's tomb.

Like many of New Orleans' historic sites, Saint Louis Cemetery No. 1 can be a dangerous place to visit, especially for people walking alone at night. The tour guides who conduct cemetery tours in New Orleans claim that people have more to fear from the living than the dead.

Old Ursuline Convent

The first group of Ursuline nuns arrived in New Orleans in 1727, only nine years after the city was founded by Jean Baptiste Le Moyne. At the time, the new city, which was populated with a multitude of gamblers, drunkards and prostitutes, was in dire need of the nuns' educational and healing skills. Construction of the convent, which was designed by Ignace Francois Broutin and built by Michael Seringue, was begun in 1726 and completed in 1733. The convent was built in the brick-between-post style, which was the primary form of construction for most of the buildings in New Orleans at the time. However, the stucco-covered building was unsuitable for New Orleans' humid climate, so plans for a new convent were initiated in 1745. The present structure, which was also designed by Broutin, was finished in 1751. A few features of the original convent, such as the winding stairway, were incorporated in the new building. The second incarnation of the Ursuline Convent served primarily as an orphanage. The infirmary, refectory, dormitory and classrooms were located on the first floor; the second floor, which was reserved for the nuns, contained an infirmary, storeroom and bedrooms for the nuns. Between 1825 and 1830, the gatehouse and the entrance portico were added by the bishop. The Ursuline Convent has withstood the ravages of the city's turbulent history, which included the devastating fires of 1788 and 1794, a local French rebellion against Spanish rule in 1768, the War of 1812, the Civil War and several hurricanes.

Stories of supernatural activity at the convent began not long after the arrival of the "casket girls" in the early 1700s. These were young girls from French convents who were sent to Louisiana to become suitable wives for the respectable men of New Orleans. Locals named the young women "casket girls" after the coffin-shaped chests they carried with them to the convent. The small caskets contained the girls' personal belongings. Legend has it that after the girls arrived at the convent, their trousseau chests were stored on the third floor and not returned to their owners until they were married. Because the girls were cloistered away in the convent until they had found suitable husbands, rumors spread about the contents of the coffins.

The spirits of nuns have been seen walking between the first and second floors of the Old Ursuline Convent. *Courtesy of the Library of Congress.*

Some people said that the coffins carried the corpses of aborted babies. Others whispered tales of vampires smuggled into New Orleans inside the coffins. To provide proof of the vampire theory, people pointed to the attic shutters that were nailed shut. The vampire stories were given new life by author Anne Rice, who mentioned the Old Ursuline Convent in her novel *Memnoch the Devil.* Even as late as the 1970s, people were spreading the story of two young paranormal investigators who hid in the courtyard of the Old Ursuline Convent just before closing time. As soon as the tour guides had left, the ghost hunters emerged from their hiding places. They then made their way up to the third floor of the convent with the intention of photographing the entities that were said to be held captive there. The bodies of the investigators were found the next morning with two puncture marks in each of their necks.

Ghosts have also been sighted inside the Old Ursuline Convent. Tourists have sensed the residual spirits of nuns walking between the first and second floors. Witnesses have described the nuns as wearing black habits with rosaries tied around their waists. Some of the more sensitive visitors claim to have detected the presence of the nuns in the nine rooms on the first floor. They have also tuned in to the misery of sick and dying children on the first floor. People waiting outside of the Old Ursuline Convent have sighted the ghost of a tall man wearing a blue uniform walking through the gardens.

In his book *The Ghosts of New Orleans*, Dr. Larry Montsz provides an account of an investigation he conducted inside the Old Ursuline Covent in the 1990s. The clairvoyants Dr. Montz brought with him claimed to have seen the spirits of nuns dressed in black habits tending to the needs of small, crying children dressed in ragged clothing. The clairvoyants also described a large procession of nuns and priests wearing hats walking through the front yard, facing the Mississippi River. At the time, no one involved in the investigation knew about a similar procession that took place at the convent in 1752. When the group began their walk-through in the attic, which is now used for storage and is off limits to the general public, one of the instigators said that he felt someone standing behind him, looking over his shoulder.

Today, the Old Ursuline Convent is the oldest surviving example of French Colonial architecture in New Orleans, as well as the oldest building in the Mississippi River Valley. It was declared a National Historic Landmark in 1960. In the 1970s, the old building was restored at a cost of $3 million. The Old Ursuline Convent and St. Mary's Church are operated as museums. Tours are given Monday through Saturday from 10:00 a.m. until 4:00 p.m. The Old Ursuline Convent has also been used as storage space for the Catholic Archives records dating back to 1718. The mystery of what exactly is stored on the attic floor of the Old Ursuline Convent has provided material for tour guides and writers for decades.

Antoine's Restaurant

Antoine's at 713 St. Louis Street is the oldest family-run restaurant in the United States. It was established by twenty-seven-year-old Antoine Alciatore, who moved to New Orleans from New York in 1840. He had worked a short while in the kitchen of the St. Charles Hotel before opening a pension—a combination boardinghouse and restaurant—just a block from the restaurant's present location on St. Louis Street. Shortly after his pension was open for business in 1840, Antoine's fiancée and her sister made the journey from New York to New Orleans. Antoine's fine French cuisine and excellent service attracted so many customers that he moved his restaurant to its present location in 1868. By the 1870s, Antoine's health had declined to the point that he was certain he did not have long to live. In 1874, Antoine left his wife in charge of the restaurant and returned to France. He died in Marseilles just a year later.

In 1875, just a few weeks after his father died, Jules Alciatore became apprenticed to his mother in the restaurant. A few months later, Jules moved to France, where he became a master chef by working in some of the finest restaurants in the country. After returning to New Orleans in 1887, Jules worked as a chef at the Pickwick Club for a while before his mother invited him to work at the family's restaurant. Jules honed his newly acquired skills at his father's restaurant, creating delicious dishes that amazed even the city's most demanding gourmets. Jules's most famous dish was Oysters Rockefeller, whose name is derived from its rich sauce.

Once he had begun to establish himself as one of the city's premier chefs, Jules married Althea Roy, the daughter of a planter from Youngsville. The couple had two children: Marie Louise, who became the grand dame of the family, and Roy Louis, who operated the restaurant until his death in 1972 at the age of seventy. Roy's son, Roy Jr., became the proprietor of Antoine's in 1975. Roy Jr. was replaced in 1984 by Marie Louise's son, Bernard "Randy" Guste, the present owner. Today, the fifth-generation-owned restaurant is known for its culinary creations, its period atmosphere and its hauntings.

Some people have speculated that each succeeding generation of owners has maintained Antoine Alciatore's high standards because he is still around, at least in spirit. Customers and employees have been describing encounters with the old man's ghost for over a century. In his book *Haunted New Orleans*, author Troy Taylor tells the story of a member of the Alciatore family who was standing outside of the Japanese Room when he saw a male figure wearing a tuxedo enter the room. He did not recognize the person, so he started to follow him into the Japanese Room but was surprised to find that the door was locked. He unlocked the door and walked into the room. He realized that he had seen a ghost when he was unable to find anyone in the room. The door he had entered was the only exit from the room.

On another occasion, one of Antoine's relatives was climbing the stairs to an office on the upper floor. In his arms were a number of important papers. The young man stopped dead in his tracks when he beheld a glowing figure standing on the landing. The apparition's facial features were completely indiscernible. Within a matter of seconds, the specter had vanished.

Antoine's spirit has also been seen in the Mystery Room, which housed an illegal bar during Prohibition. Guests entered the bar through a secret door leading from the ladies' restroom. When asked how they got the drinks in their hands, they would say, "It's a mystery to me." One day, a young employee noticed a man he assumed was the headwaiter walk into the Mystery Room. The young man followed the male figure into the room because he had a question to ask him. The employee was baffled when he could find no sign of the headwaiter. When he finally located the headwaiter in a different part of the restaurant, he asked him where he had gone. The headwaiter replied that he had not been in the Mystery Room. The confused employee described the man he had seen walk into the Mystery Room. The headwaiter listened carefully to the young man's detailed description and then informed him that he had seen the ghost of Antoine Alciatore.

According to Jeff Dwyer, author of *Ghost Hunter's Guide to New Orleans*, several other ghosts have been sighted in Antoine's. Guests and staff members have seen people dressed in nineteenth-century clothing passing through the restaurant. Disembodied faces occasionally appear in the mirrors in the men's and the ladies' rooms. Cold spots have been detected throughout the building. A transparent figure dressed in a tuxedo has been spotted in the dining room.

The past is present everywhere in Antoine's. The 1840 Room has been converted into a museum of sorts where one can find oddities such as a cookbook published in Paris in 1659 and a great silver duck press. The walls are lined with photographs of celebrities who have dined in the restaurant, including Calvin Coolidge, Rex Harrison, Franklin Roosevelt, Bob Hope, Bing Crosby and Pope John Paul II. The most enduring remnant of the past, however, seems to be the spirit of the founder of the restaurant, Antoine Alciatore.

Saint Louis Cathedral

Saint Louis Cathedral is the most imposing building in Jackson Square. Churches have stood on this location since 1718, when a wooden structure was erected by the city's first colonists. The Church of St. Louis, as it was known back then, was replaced by a brick-and-timber church, which was completed in 1727. The Great Fire of 1788, which consumed many of New Orleans' wooden buildings, also destroyed the Church of St. Louis and the priests' residence. By the next year, the debris from the previous church had been cleared away, and construction of a new cathedral had begun. The next incarnation of the Church of St. Louis was completed in December 1794. In 1819, Ben Henry Latrobe, the designer of the White House, created the central bell tower. The bell and clock were brought to New Orleans by a local clockmaker named Jean Delachaux. An organ was installed in 1829. In 1849, an Irish builder named John Patrick Kirwan was hired to expand the aging structure in order to accommodate the cathedral's growing congregation. The extensive renovation of the church involved demolishing everything except for the towers on the front façade and the lateral walls. In 1850, construction was going as planned when suddenly the central tower collapsed. The present cathedral, which contains very little of the Spanish Colonial structure, was finished in 1850. In 1964, Pope Paul VI designated Saint Louis Cathedral as a minor basilica. Today, the parish includes over six thousand members, as well as a few very well-known ghosts.

One of the ghosts that occasionally makes his presence known at Saint Louis Cathedral is the spirit of Père Dagobert. He moved to New Orleans in 1745 to serve as pastor of the Church of St. Louis. He immediately endeared himself to the sick and the poor of New Orleans by putting their needs at the top of his list of priorities. The relatively placid lives of his parishioners were shaken to their cores in October 1764, when the governor of Louisiana ceded New Orleans to Spain. Six men from prominent families in New Orleans soon began organizing a revolt against Spain. Resistance against Spain escalated to the point that in March 1766, the first Spanish governor, Don Antoio de Ulloa, fled to Havana. Spain retaliated by sending a fleet of twenty-four ships to New Orleans to put down the rebellion. After the leaders of the rebellion were arrested, the commander of the fleet, an Irish expatriate named Don Alejandro O'Reilly, condemned them to death by firing squad in the spot where the Old U.S. Mint stands today. Following the execution, O'Reilly refused to permit the corpses of the fallen resistance leaders to be buried. Instead, their bodies were left to rot and fester in the sun outside the Spanish garrison in order to discourage anyone else from even thinking about rebelling against the Spanish regime. Eventually, Père Dagobert's resentment at O'Reilly's desecration of the bodies of the slain Frenchmen, all of whom were Catholic, became too much for him to bear. One night, he invited the families of the six men to meet him at the cathedral. The dead men's relatives were surprised to find the bodies of their loved ones lying outside of the church. Flanked by Père Etienne and Père Hypolite, Père Dagobert sang the funeral mass in the pouring rain. Afterward, the funeral procession carried the bodies to St. Louis Cemetery No. 1, where they were secretly buried.

Today, many people claim to have heard Père Dagobert's beautiful voice singing the Kyrie on rainy nights just outside of the cathedral. His ghost has also been known to sing the Kyrie before the high altar of the cathedral after closing hours. Sometimes on rainy nights, people spot Père Dagobert's spectral form praying on the altar steps.

Another Capuchin monk whose spirit occasionally makes his presence known at Saint Louis Cathedral is Père Antoine, whose Spanish name was Antonio de Sedella. When he first stepped off the boat from Spain, he was intent on setting up an American version of the Court of Inquisition, focusing primarily on the Creoles. However, by the time Père Antoine had become pastor of Saint Louis Cathedral, his mission in life had shifted to ministering to the needs of the poor living in his parish. He founded an outreach program for prisoners, the poor and slaves. Protestants, as well as Catholics, benefited from Père Anthony's ministry during the city's outbreaks of yellow fever. During his tenure as pastor of Saint Louis Cathedral, Père Anthony also baptized Marie Laveau and performed her wedding ceremony. When he died in January 1829, the entire city mourned. However, many residents of New Orleans are convinced that his love for his city did not end with his death.

Père Dagobert's sad, sweet singing voice has been heard outside of Saint Louis Cathedral on rainy nights. *Courtesy of the author.*

For over a century, people have reported seeing the ghostly, black-robed figure of the good monk walking down the small alley that bears his name, Père Antoine's Alley. Père Antoine's apparition is most commonly sighted early in the morning. Late one evening, a woman wearing high heels was walking down Père Antoine's Alley when she suddenly lost her balance. She fell into the arms of a black-robed man, who appeared to be as surprised as she was. When she turned around to thank him, the man was gone. On wintry afternoons, his apparition has been sighted walking through the Cathedral garden. As a rule, the specter is seen reading a book, quite probably a book of prayer, just as he did when he was alive. Père Antoine's ghost appears inside the cathedral only during the Christmas Vigil Midnight Mass. He is usually seen walking on the left side of the altar with a candle in his hands.

Jackson Barracks Military Museum

Jackson Barracks was established in 1834, based on plans drawn up by Second Lieutenant Frederick Wilkinson. At the time, the New Orleans Barracks, as it was known then, consisted of fifteen Greek Revival buildings surrounded by a brick masonry-walled enceinte. Towers were built at each of the four corners of the enceinte. A sally port at the front of the barracks led to a wharf on the river. According to an article appearing in the *Times-Democrat* in 1914, the post was considered "the finest arrangement and setting of purely colonial architecture in the country." In 1836, the New Orleans Barracks was used as a point of embarkation for as many as 250 Native Americans during the Trail of Tears campaign. A Seminole chief named Jumper died at the New Orleans Barracks. In 1845, troops under the command of General Zachary Taylor organized and funneled supplies at the New Orleans Barracks. During the Mexican War, sick and wounded soldiers were treated at the base. After New Orleans was captured by Federal troops on April 30, 1862, the post was used as a temporary quarters for Union troops. Toward the end of the Civil War, the base was used as a field hospital. On July 7, 1856, New Orleans Barracks was officially renamed Jackson Barracks in honor of Andrew Jackson, the military hero of the Battle of New Orleans. In 1869, two black regiments, the Thirty-ninth and Fortieth, were stationed at Jackson Barracks.

The military considered Jackson Barracks to be strategically unimportant for the next twenty-five years. Improvements in the post were made in 1905 after the Spanish-American War. In 1921, the Louisiana National Guard used Jackson Barracks as its base of operations. The Louisiana adjutant general used Jackson Barracks as his headquarters in 1931. Works Progress Administration (WPA) workers made considerable improvements in the post between 1936 and 1841, including the replacement of rotted wood and slate roofs. The federal government again took possession of Jackson Barracks in 1941 at the start of World War II. After the war, the Louisiana National Guard returned to Jackson Barracks in 1946. Nine years later, the State of Louisiana acquired Jackson Barracks, which was placed on the National Register of Historic Places in 1976. Throughout the twentieth and twenty-first centuries, the preservation of the Jackson Barracks has been a struggle. However, one feature of the old base that does not seem to be in danger of fading away is its ghost story.

The Washington Artillery armory at Jackson Barracks was built in 1970 on the site of the old polo field, where a tragic execution of sorts took place. By the 1930s, horses were being phased out by the military because of the emphasis being placed on mechanized artillery. In 1937, horses that had been used to pull the caissons and wagons of the Washington Artillery at the Jackson Barracks were transferred to other duties. The twenty-one horses that were designated as being too old to be of any use by the military were slated to be "put down." In June of that year, the old horses were taken out to the polo field and shot. One of the soldiers who stood by and watched the grisly act was thirty-six-year-old First Sergeant Henry Brunig, who had taken care of the horses that pulled the artillery pieces. The day after the execution, Brunig walked into the barracks warehouse, placed a pistol to his head and pulled the trigger.

At the time, many people, including newspaper reporters, assumed that the supply sergeant who had been responsible for everything the horses needed, from harnesses to horseshoes, had taken his own life out of grief for the noble steeds that had served the military well for so many years. However, people who were close to Sergeant Brunig believed that his personal problems might have driven him to commit this rash act. National Guard official Edward Benezech, whose father was one of Brunig's superior officers, said that Brunig "had some other problems," which probably included strife among family members.

Ever since the Washington Artillery armory opened in 1970, soldiers began reporting strange occurrences. Many soldiers of the 141st Battalion of the Washington Artillery said that they heard weird noises inside the building. One of these soldiers was First Sergeant Terry Donelson, who told a reporter named Steve Cannizaro about some of the strange sounds he had been hearing since he was first stationed at Jackson Barracks in 1982. "I swear I would hear doors slamming, toilets flushing. You would hear water running," Donelson said. He went on to say that personnel who worked late also heard unnerving sounds in the armory: "People would swear they heard people walking when they knew they were alone."

Jackson Barracks was extensively renovated after suffering heavy damage by Hurricane Katrina in 2005. As a result of the destruction the base suffered after being submerged in up to twenty-two feet of water, many of the oldest buildings had to be razed. Nevertheless, the restored portions of the old post look the same as they did in the 1840s. Evidence exists, though, that the restoration process might be responsible for the escalated levels of paranormal activity inside the museum. Caretakers and staff members have not only been hearing the usual noises, but they have also seen phantom soldiers walking through the building.

The Lanaux Mansion

The Lanaux Mansion at 547 Esplanade Avenue was built in 1870 by Charles Andrew Johnson, a well-to-do lawyer. When Johnson was not practicing law, he was poring through art books and magazines in search of color schemes and furnishings for his twelve-thousand-square-foot mansion. Because Johnson did not have a wife or children, he was able to devote most of his spare time to making his home the showplace of New Orleans. Johnson bequeathed the home to his partner's daughter, Marie Andry, on his deathbed in 1896. People said that he had fallen deeply in love with Marie, even though she was married and had a child. Generations of the Lanaux family, including a wealthy merchant named Pierre Lanaux, continued to own and live in the mansion until 1953. The current owner, Ruth Bodenheimer, fell in love with the old house when she was seventeen years old. She purchased the house and began restoring it in the early 1980s. She returned as many of the home's original furnishings as she could find, including Johnson's portrait.

Ruth insists that she could not have replicated the home's original color scheme without a little help from beyond the grave. In his book *Ghost Hunter's Guide to New Orleans*, author Jeff Dwyer says that when she was trying to decide on the perfect style of wallpaper or the correct style of draperies, something urged her to peruse Johnson's collection of books and magazines. Soon, she found the answer to her question in Johnson's penciled-in marginalia or in underlined passages.

The Lanaux Mansion is now one of New Orleans' most fashionable bed-and-breakfasts. The picturesque old home has been featured in a number of films. For example, the lobby and exterior were used in *The Curious Case of Benjamin Button* (2007). Ruth Bodenheimer was reluctant to allow the crew to film scenes throughout the house for fear that they might damage some of the antiques. If the crew had had access to the entire house, they might have captured the ghostly image of Charles Andrew Johnson, which has been known to walk through the mansion in a black morning coat.

The Cornstalk Hotel

One of the most photographed buildings in the French Quarter is the Cornstalk Hotel. The site on which it was built in the early 1800s had been occupied by a number of older dwellings, all of which were destroyed by the various fires that ravaged the city in the eighteenth century. Judge François Xavier Martin lived here between 1816 and 1826. He achieved fame as the first chief justice of the Louisiana State Court and as the author of the first history of Louisiana. One of the most illustrious visitors to the mansion in the early nineteenth century was Harriet Beecher Stowe. The story goes that she was staying at the house when she visited New Orleans' infamous slave market. Her revulsion at the bartering and selling of human beings inspired her, some believe, to write *Uncle Tom's Cabin*.

Despite the fact that a number of famous people have stayed at the Cornstalk Hotel, including Elvis Presley in 1957, the fine old house is best known for its ornate fence. Two legends have arisen to explain its origin. In the more romantic of the two tales, one of the early owners of the house brought his new bride from Iowa to live in this splendid home in the heart of the French Quarter. To make her feel more at home in the most exotic city in the Deep South, her husband instructed a local artisan to create a wrought-iron fence in the likeness of a corn field.

The second version of the story is far more realistic. A wealthy man had a mistress who demanded that she be given duplicates of everything he had given his wife. When he built his wife a mansion in the Garden District with a cornstalk fence, he had to build another version of the same house in the French Quarter for his mistress.

Aside from being conveniently located on Royal Street, the Cornstalk Inn has a strong attraction to lovers of the paranormal because of its ghost stories. The apparitions of children occasionally run through the hallways.

The sounds of childish laughter and spectral footsteps resound through the building at times. So many ghostly encounters have been reported at the Cornstalk Hotel that even the most cynical employees have become believers after a while. For example, in the early 2000s, a desk clerk had not worked the front desk for very long before he began hearing about the ghost stories. He brushed them off as the imaginings of impressionable minds—until he witnessed doors opening and closing by themselves. Late one evening, he heard a tapping on the office door. When he discovered that no one was standing in the hallway, chills ran up his spine. Ghosts are indeed a harsh reality at the Cornstalk Hotel.

The Hermann-Grima House

The Hermann-Grima House was built in 1831 at 820 St. Louis Street for a wealthy Creole man, Sam Hermann, and his wife and children. The Grima family moved in around the turn of the century. In 1924, an organization called the Christian Woman's Exchange, which was founded in 1881, purchased the Hermann-Grima House to provide single women with a place where they could live safely in a chaperoned environment. In the late 1960s, the Christian Woman's Exchange shifted its focus to historical preservation and education and transformed the Federal-style mansion into a house museum. The organization's mission was to fill the Hermann-Grima House with exhibits and artifacts from the "Golden Age of New Orleans." The elegant old house is furnished with the original mahogany dining table; portraits of two of Sam's children, Lucien and Marie Virginia; and etched hurricane shades donated by descendants of the Grima family. The home was designated as a National Historic Landmark in 1974.

The Hermann-Grima House is an architectural treasure. It has the only functional outdoor kitchen in the French Quarter. The docents who guide tourists through the house also believe that the ghosts of the Hermann and Grima families must be pleased with the Christian Woman's Exchange's preservation efforts because the pleasant smells of rose and lavender occasionally waft through the building. On the other hand, the spirits could also have been revived by the October thematic tours, during which the home is decorated as if the occupants are in mourning.

The Bourbon-Orleans Hotel

In 1817, a far-sighted businessman named John Davis built the Orleans Ballroom to capitalize on the thriving social scene in New Orleans. Before long, some of the Crescent City's most prestigious social events, such as carnival balls and masquerades, were being held at the Orleans Ballroom. Ten years later, the state and house legislative meetings were held at the Orleans Ballroom as well. According to local legend, Andrew Jackson was addressing a large gathering of the Democratic-Republican Party inside the Orleans Ballroom when he announced his candidacy for the presidency of the United States of America.

In 1881, the same building that had been used for quadroon balls and coming-out parties was converted into a convent. The new owners, the Sisters of the Holy Family, operated an orphanage and school inside the convent. The African American nuns worked, prayed and taught inside the building until 1924, when they moved to their new home in New Orleans East. In 1964, a local developer purchased the entire block. One year later, the Bourbon Orleans Hotel was housed in the old building where beautiful women had glided across the dance floors and saintly nuns had ministered to their young charges. Some people say that they still do.

Testimony from guests and staff over the years indicates that between fifteen and twenty ghosts could be roaming the halls of the Bourbon-Orleans Hotel. The ghost of a Confederate soldier has been seen roaming around the corridors of the third and sixth floors. A spectral dancer has been seen twirling beneath the ballroom's magnificent crystal chandelier. In the same room, people have heard rustling sounds from behind the draperies. It seemed, according to witnesses, that someone was trying unsuccessfully to hide.

The most poignant spirits inside the hotel are quite possibly remnants of one of the yellow fever epidemics that claimed hundreds of lives in New Orleans in the nineteenth century. During these tragic times, the nuns turned their convent into a medical ward. The ghosts of small children and mournful women manifest themselves throughout the hotel. Phantom footsteps have been heard on all of the floors. The most frequently sighted children's ghost is the apparition of a little girl who has been seen rolling a ball down the hallway on the sixth floor.

The Bourbon-Orleans Hotel has changed considerably since it was first built. The last major renovation cost over $1 million. Despite the owners' best efforts to bring the old building into the modern age, the past keeps surfacing in dark corridors and shadowy corners.

Muriel's Jackson Square

In 1718, a French Canadian named Claude Trepagnier built a modest cottage on a tract of land that eventually became part of Jackson Square. Trepagnier's house was used as a stopping point for slaves just before they were auctioned off at the New Orleans slave market. In 1745, the royal treasurer of French Louisiana colonies, Jean Baptiste Destrehan, purchased the property. His son inherited the house and land in 1765 following Jean's death. In 1776, Pierre Phillipe de Marigny bought the cottage, which he used as a town house when he made one of his frequent excursions to New Orleans from his plantation just outside of town. On March 21, 1788, Marigny's house was severely damaged in the same fire that had destroyed 856 buildings in the French Quarter, including the army barracks, the municipal building and the original Cabildo, which was the seat of colonial government in New Orleans.

In 1789, Pierre Antoine Lepardi Jourdan built an impressive mansion on the site of Marigny's dwelling. Jourdan was so attached to his home that when he lost the house in a poker game in 1814, he walked up the stairs to his room on the second floor and shot himself. After the Civil War, a number of different people owned the building. For a while, the mansion became one of the French Quarter's best bordellos. Today, the old house is an upscale restaurant called Muriel's Jackson Square. With some encouragement, the waitstaff might serve up ghost stories along with the local fare.

Muriel's Jackson Square is said to be haunted by a host of ghosts. Jourdan manifests himself as a glimmer of sparkling lights inside the Inner Séance Lounge. Customers seated inside the lounge have heard strange knocking sounds emanating from the bricks. For several consecutive nights in 2001, glasses that had been arranged behind the bar propelled themselves twelve feet through the air and shattered against a wall. Footsteps are occasionally heard on the second floor. During an investigation conducted by a group of paranormal investigators, members encountered shadowy figures and disembodied voices. The voice of a female is heard, as a rule, when women are present.

The staff members at Muriel's Jackson Square have never really felt threatened by their "special guests." In fact, they feel very comfortable around their spirits and are glad to have them around. Perhaps this is the reason why a special table is always reserved for Mr. Jourdan, complete with bread and wine.

The Provincial Hotel

Located in the heart of the French Quarter, the Provincial Hotel consists of several different buildings. The two-story 300 Building surrounds a courtyard that was used as a medicinal herb garden for a military hospital a few blocks away. An ice company once owned the 100 and 200 Buildings. In the 400 Building, which was constructed in the 1830s, a store was housed on the first floor.

Most of the paranormal activity in the hotel takes place in the 500 Building, which is located on the site of a structure that was once owned by the Ursuline nuns. They arrived in New Orleans in 1725. For the previous three years, the building had been used as a hospital. During the Battle of New Orleans in 1814, the building was converted into a military hospital where both American and British soldiers were treated. In the 1830s, a lawyer named Dominique Seghers bought the Ursuline hospital. Seghers tore down the old hospital and replaced it with two new buildings. In the 1850s, the new owner transformed the two buildings into a boardinghouse. He reserved part of the building for shops. A wide hallway connected the two buildings. During the Civil War, the conjoined buildings served as a military hospital. After a fire destroyed the two buildings in 1874, a new structure was built in their place. The Renter Seed Company was housed there for a while.

In 1961, the Depepe family began acquiring various buildings with the intention of combining them into a luxury hotel. The 500 Building was purchased in 1969. Guests and employees of the hotel could tell that this particular building was "different" not long after it opened. They began to notice bloodstains that would suddenly appeared on the floor and the sheets and then vanish entirely after a few seconds. The ghostly figures of doctors with bloodstained aprons have been seen strolling through the corridors, as if they are making their rounds. Spectral soldiers swathed in bandages hobble around on crutches in the courtyard or bask in the shade. A young female nurse has been sighted walking down a staircase. Moans and cries have been heard throughout the hotel.

A number of guests have had some very unnerving experiences inside the old hotel. One guest opened the door to her room and beheld a grisly sight. A soldier, his face contorted in pain and his uniform splotched with blood, was twisting and rolling on the bed. In another instance, a woman who had been watching the Mardi Gras parade returned to her room and fell asleep. Suddenly, she felt a pair of large, strong hands yank her off the bed and drag her across the floor. On another occasion, a bellboy who had just led a couple to their room unlocked the door; the trio was shocked to see a man wearing a 1930s khakis uniform, festooned with medals, standing at attention. After a few seconds, the figure slowly faded away.

One of the spirits in the hotel seems to be a fan of country music. If a guest has the radio on a rock or rap station, the tuner moves to a local country station on its own. One night, when a séance was held in this particular room, a tape recorder captured a male voice saying, "Please, tell Diane I have to go" and "I have to leave."

Most of the ghosts haunting the 500 Building are probably residual spirits that are going through their daily routines. It is also possible, though, that a sense of duty has compelled the spirits of the soldiers, the doctors and the nurses to return to the building that had served as a hospital for almost 150 years.

LaLaurie House

Marie Delphine Macarty was one of five children born to Louis Barthelemy Chevalier de Macarty and Marie Jeanne Lovable Macarty, two of New Orleans' most respected citizens. She was married on June 11, 1800, at St. Louis Cathedral. Her husband, Don Ramon de Lopez y Angula, was a native of Regino, Galicia, Spain. He was appointed Spanish consul general to the territory that had just been acquired as part of the Louisiana Purchase. Four years later, Angula died while traveling from Havana to Madrid. A few days later, Delphine gave birth to a daughter, Marie Delphine Borja Lopez y Angula de Candelaria. After learning of her husband's death, Delphine and her baby returned to New Orleans. She remarried on June 16, 1808, this time to Jean Blanque, a lawyer, legislator and merchant. The couple moved into a fine home at 409 Royal Street. Four children were born to Delphine and Jean during their marriage. Following his death in 1816, she remained a widow until marrying her third husband, Dr. Leonard Luis Nicolas LaLaurie, on June 12, 1825. The handsome couple soon became fixtures in New Orleans' social scene in the early 1830s. They built a luxurious mansion befitting their high social status at 1140 Royal Street in 1832. The parties that they threw in their home were high points on the city's social calendar for the next two years.

The possibility that this refined husband and wife harbored a deep, dark secret never occurred to most of the people who drank their liquor and ate their hors d'ouvres. However, a few people began to suspect that things

The LaLaurie House is said to be haunted by the ghosts of the slaves Delphine LaLaurie tortured and mutilated. *Courtesy of the author.*

were not exactly right in the mansion when one of their neighbors saw Madame LaLauire chasing a young slave girl across the rooftop with a whip. The neighbor reported to the authorities that the girl slid off the roof and fell to her death on the flagstones. As punishment for breaking a local law forbidding the mistreatment of slaves, the LaLauries had all of their slaves removed by the police. Not accustomed to living in a house without servants, Madame LaLaurie and Luis asked their relatives to buy the couple's slaves and sell them back to them. Only a few of Madame LaLaurie's friends and neighbors believed her story that the death of her personal servant was a horrible accident.

The truth behind the rumors that had been circulating about the LaLauries became readily apparent on April 10, 1834, when clouds of smoke billowed from the kitchen area. One of their neighbors, M. Montreuil, knocked on the door and asked Madame LaLaurie if he could help put out the fire, but she told him to mind his own business and slammed the door in his face. Montreuil retreated to the crowd that was forming outside the house and told one of the bystanders, Judge Canonge, that he was concerned for the safety of the slaves within the house. Montreuil, the judge, a man named Fernandez and several volunteer firemen broke into the mansion to save as many people as they could. They found an aged female slave in the kitchen who had set the fire in the hope that she would be rescued from her captivity. A locked door prevented the men from entering the upper room of the house, so they decided to search through the attic instead. As soon as they opened the wooden door, they reeled from the foul stench of death and decomposition. More than a dozen slaves were chained to the walls. Human organs and amputated body parts littered the floor. One slave woman was caged like an animal. Her limbs had been broken and reset at strange angles, lending her the appearance of a large crab. Another woman was nothing more than a head and a torso, her limbs having been surgically removed. Protruding from a hole in the head of a male slave, shackled to the floor, was a stick that had been used to stir his brains. Another male slave had his genitalia removed, apparently in a crude attempt to change his sex. Other men were blinded and had various body parts cut off. The publisher of the *New Orleans Bee*, Jerome Bayon, tried to capture the horror of the scene in an article published on April 11, 1834, when he wrote, "Seven slaves, more or less horribly mutilated, were seen suspended by the neck, with their limbs apparently stretched and torn from one extremity to the other…We feel confident that the community will share with us our indignation and that vengeance will fall heavily upon the guilty culprit."

The poetic justice that the outraged public demanded did not come to pass. Shortly after the fire had been put out, Delphine and her husband sneaked back into the house and threw as many valuables as they could into their carriage. A few minutes later, the couple barreled their carriage through the throng of people who were brandishing hangman's nooses and screaming epithets. The specific details of their escape have become the stuff of legend. In one version of the story, they drove their carriage down Bayou Road and boarded a ship bound for Mandeville. While they were there, Delphine granted power of attorney to her son-in-law, Placide Forstall, in New Orleans in order that the couple's affairs would be put in order. From Mandeville, they took another ship to the port city of Mobile and eventually traveled to Paris, France. In another variant, the LaLauries hid out in New Orleans for a few days, leaving only when it became painfully clear that public opinion was decidedly against them.

As soon as the LaLauries fled New Orleans, the mob took out its anger on their home. They ripped the curtains, threw a piano out of one of the upper windows, tore up the featherbeds and carried off expensive paintings and furniture. Once the house was emptied of its furnishings, the crowd attacked the house itself, ripping banisters from stairways and pulling doors off their hinges. The scene of so many unspeakable crimes stood abandoned for three years. What had once been one of the city's grandest showplaces had become a shunned house.

Suspicions that the LaLaurie Mansion was haunted arose soon after other people moved in. In 1837, the mansion was renovated by Pierre Edouard Trastour, who added a third floor. He did not live in the house for very long before selling it to Charles Caffin. A few months later, the murder house changed hands again when it was purchased by the widow of Horace Cammack in 1862. People living nearby attributed the string of successive owners to the screams that echoed throughout the house late at night. Rumors spread about the ghosts of slaves appearing on the balconies. The most common sighting was that of a wild-haired, frenzied woman brandishing a whip and chasing a slave girl across the roof.

Soon after the Civil War, the LaLaurie mansion was converted into an integrated school for girls from the Lower District. In 1874, the black girls were expelled by the "White League," a white paramilitary group that tried to prevent freed slaves from voting. The house with the evil reputation was turned into a music conservatory in 1882. In the early 1890s, the spacious mansion became a boardinghouse for Italian immigrants, one of whom claimed to have encountered the ghost of a large black man as he wearily made his way up the stairs one night after work. The muscular slave, bound with chains, blocked the Italian's way. The Italian attempted to grab the black man and throw him aside, but the strange figure vanished before his eyes. Other tenants came home to find their pets decapitated and their mules chopped up. Crying children told their parents that they had been chased by a crazy lady with a blood-soaked whip.

Between 1893 and 1916, an Italian immigrant operated a saloon on the first floor of the house. In 1932, a furniture dealer ran his business from the LaLaurie house for a short time. One morning, the owner opened the door and was appalled by what he saw. The furniture and walls were covered in a dark, noxious liquid. Thinking that his merchandise had been ruined by vandals, he locked himself inside the store one night with a shotgun. The house was so still that he soon fell asleep. When he awoke the next morning, all of the chairs and tables were soaked with smelly goo. He immediately closed up his business and left for good.

During the Great Depression, William J. Warrenton, a wealthy philanthropist, housed indigent men in the old building. People said that many of these homeless men never spent more than a single night in the house. They seemed to prefer living in the wide outdoors to rooming with restless spirits.

In 1976 and 1980, the LaLaurie mansion was restored by the architectural firm of Koch and Williams. Actor Nicholas Cage raised eyebrows—and made headlines—when he purchased the estate anonymously for $3.45 million through the Hancock Real Estate Agency. Cage, who has confessed to a lifelong interest in the paranormal, told a reporter that several groups of paranormal investigators had asked him for permission to investigate his house, but he refused out of respect for the spirits inside the house. He lost the house to foreclosure in 2009, and it was sold at auction to the Regions Financial Corporation. A few people who were familiar with the house's bloody legacy surmised that Cage was the victim of some sort of curse that has befallen many of the people who were bold—or foolish—enough to buy it.

The Columns Hotel

In 1883, famed New Orleans architect Thomas Sully designed a fine mansion for Simon Hernsheim in the upper Garden District. He was the owner of Hernsheim Brothers and Company, the largest maker of cigars in the United States. The house passed out of the Hernsheim family in 1898 following the death of Simon Hernsheim in 1898. A number of different people owned the mansion in the early twentieth century. After a few decades, it became a boardinghouse. In 1980, Claire and Jacques Creppel bought the old house and immediately undertook an ambitious restoration project. Today, the old Hernsheim mansion is the Columns Hotel. The house holds the distinction of being the only remaining mansion of a series of town houses that were designed by Thomas Sully in the 1880s. The hotel has become known for its ghosts as well.

Several different full-bodied apparitions have appeared in the Columns Hotel. Most of the sightings are of the spirit of Simon Hernsheim. Guests who have seen the ghost of the elderly gentleman feel that he is simply looking in on them before he dissipates. A less-frequently sighted spirit in the hotel is the ghost of a little girl. She has been known to cavort around the balcony, usually at night. The third ghost is of the classic variety, the lady in white. She seems to favor the garden and the ballroom.

The Columns Hotel bears a strong resemblance to the elegant mansion that Simon Hernsheim called home at the turn of the century. Many of the original furnishings remain, including a built-in breakfront and a mahogany stairwell leading up to a beautiful square-dome stained-glass skylight. The presence of so many ghosts suggests that Claire and Jacques Creppel have inadvertently made the former occupants feel at home.

Dauphin Orleans Hotel

Real estate records show that buildings have sat on this site since 1775. The Dauphin Orleans Hotel is actually composed of several buildings, all of which date back to the nineteenth century. One of these buildings is the aptly named Audubon Cottage. Between 1821 and 1822, famed naturalist John Jacob Audubon painted the illustrations for his *Birds of America* while rooming in this small structure. The Audubon Cottage is now the hotel's primary meeting room. The Dauphine Orleans Hotel also includes fourteen Patio Rooms across the street. These rooms were part of a town house built in 1834 for a rich merchant named Samuel Hermann. The hotel bar is housed in May Baily's Place, which was one of the most notorious bordellos in New Orleans' red-light district, Storyville. The hotel proudly displays a license that the bordello was issued in May 1857 to operate legally in New Orleans. The "Bordello" guest suite is located above the old bordello. A red light still illuminates the courtyard of the hotel, just as it did during the Civil War when soldiers frequented the establishment. The hotel came into being in 1969, three years after the site was purchased and the buildings were renovated. Today, the Dauphine Orleans offers guests Wi-Fi access, the daily newspaper, deluxe continental breakfast and, for a lucky few, a glimpse into the lives of past occupants of the buildings.

Both male and female spirits are said to haunt the old hotel. Most of the paranormal activity seems to emanate from those years when the bar area was used as a bordello. The ghosts of ladies of the evening have been seen dancing around. In the morning and late afternoon, bouncing activity has been observed in beds in the "Bordello" guest suite. Bartenders have opened the bar in the morning and discovered that someone—or something—has rearranged the bottles. At least one bartender believes that this is May Bailey's way of making her presence known. A male apparition has been seen as well. Witnesses describe him as a dark-haired man in a Civil War uniform who walks around the courtyard.

A number of strange reports have come from some of the rooms inside the hotel, especially Suites 110 and 111. For example, in the early 2000s, a young man named Carlos Detres had just returned to his room in the Dauphine Orleans Hotel after dining at one of the city's fine restaurants. He stuck his card key in the door and proceeded to open it. Carlos became alarmed when the door would open only a couple of inches. He closed the door, slid in his card key and tried once again to open the door. He still could open the door only enough to see darkness inside the room. Thinking that a burglar was in the room, he summoned up the courage to insert his card key into the slot once more. This time, the door opened on its own. Cautiously, he entered the room, looking for the intruder in the bathroom, inside the closet and under the bed. No one was there. The identity of the ghost responsible for these disturbances is unknown.

La Louisianne Bar and Bistro

La Louisianne Bar and Bistro is one of the oldest restaurants in New Orleans. It was built in 1837 by a merchant, James Walters Jacharie, who enjoyed entertaining at his beautiful home. In 1881, a businessman named Amaron Ledoux purchased the building and leased it out to Louis Bezaudun and his wife, Ann. They converted the private residence into a hotel and restaurant. In 1890, the Bezanduns asked Ann's nephew, Fernand Jule Alciatore, to operate the restaurant.

Over the next thirty years, La Louisiane became known as the place to go for superb French-Creole fare. Alciatore bought the restaurant in 1920. He was succeeded by his son, Fernand Jr., in 1930. Fernand Jr. died suddenly the next year, leaving the restaurant to his wife, Helen, who sold it for $200,000 to the firm A.M. and J. Solari Ltd. of New Orleans. In 1933, the owner of the firm, Omar H. Cheer, closed La Louisane temporarily and set about making the restaurant cleaner and more efficient. It reopened a few months later but closed again in 1942, flowing Cheer's death. In 1943, three business partners—Edward H. Sellers, Leon Dupont and Harold E. Wise—leased the building for $150,000 and reopened the restaurant under a new name: Restaurant and Lounge de la Louisiane. In 1954, the restaurant's original name was restored by its new owner, "Diamond Jim" Moran, who added the Diamond Room and the Flamingo Crystal Room. Four years later, he died from a heart attack. His two sons took over La Louisiane and continued running it until 1978, when they turned over the operation of the restaurant to Salvador and Joseph Marcello. Between 1978 and 1980, the Marcello brothers transformed La Louisiane into a popular Italian-Creole restaurant.

Jim Chehardy and Caroll Glindmeyer ran the restaurant between 1993 in 1996, when it closed. La Lousianne did not reopen until 2004, after it was completely renovated by the present owners, the Smith family. Today, La Louisianne Bar and Bistro proudly showcases its long history, parts of which seem to "come alive" at times.

One of the building's ghosts is apparently the spirit of Amaron Ledoux's wife. For many years, she opened her home to destitute women who otherwise would probably have resorted to prostitution to survive. Her benevolent spirit was frequently sighted during the 1960s by the "bunnies" at the Playboy Club next door. They felt as if Mrs. LeDoux's ghost was looking out for them.

The spirits of the next owners of the restaurant, Ann and Louis Bezaudun, have been seen leaving the building. Witnesses describe them as an elegantly dressed couple from the early nineteenth century. Wearing a beautiful black dress, Ann smiles and nods at passersby before dissolving into thin air. The current owner of the restaurant, Brett Smith, had a ghostly encounter in 2004 while renovating the restaurant. He said he was on the telephone when he happened to look though the carpenter's plastic drape. Sitting on the ledge was the figure of a woman. Brett stared at the entity for a few moments, and then a cool breeze wafted over him. At the same time, the hairs of his neck stood on end. When the woman faded away, he realized that he and his family would be sharing ownership of the old restaurant. So far, the Smiths' partnership with the previous owners has been amicable.

Le Pavillon Hotel

The history of the location of Le Pavillon Hotel is just as fascinating as the history of the hotel itself. The land was originally owned by the Jesuits in the early eighteenth century. After Sieur de Bienville created the plans for the city of New Orleans in 1721, a wealthy planter named Jean Gravier acquired the property, which had been abandoned by the Jesuits when they were forced to leave. For a while, Gravier grew sugar cane and indigo on his plantation, but by the end of the eighteenth century, Gravier had lost his money, and the plantation was abandoned.

In the early 1800s, the overgrown plantation was a refuge for wild animals and outlaws. In the 1830s, the New Orleans and Carrollton Railroad purchased the land, drained and filled in the bogs and built a depot on the site where Le Pavillon Hotel now stands. After a few decades, the railroad's business declined, and the depot fell into disrepair. The new owners turned it into a venue for traveling shows and circuses. In 1867, the former depot was razed, and the National Theatre, also known as the German Theatre, was built in its place. The owner, Philip Welein, successfully resisted the city's attempts to lay claim to the land in the 1870s. In 1889, the theater burned down under suspicious circumstances. For the next decade, the legal ownership of the property was in limbo. In 1899, La Baronne Reality was allowed to buy the land and to build a hotel on the site. When the New York firm of Milliken Brothers completed construction of the building in 1907, it was given the name the New Hotel Denechaud because the owners wanted the general public to view it as a successor to the original Hotel Denechaud at the corner of Carondelet and Perdido Streets. Famed architects Toledano and Woogan incorporated features into their design that would perpetuate the previous Hotel Denechaud's reputation for luxury, such as a basement and hydraulic elevators.

Throughout the first half of the twentieth century, the new Hotel Denechaud earned a reputation as one of the grandest hotels in Louisiana. Some of the city's most prestigious social events were held here. However, by the 1960s, the old hotel was starting to show its age. In 1970, the new owner tried to restore some of the old hotel's turn-of-the-century elegance by installing marble railings from the Grand Hotel in Paris, marble statues from Italy and crystal chandeliers from Czechoslovakia. The owners also gave the hotel a new name: Le Pavillon Hotel. It was placed on the National Register of Historic Places in 1991. Modern amenities include Wi-Fi and cable television.

The past blends with the present in other ways as well at Le Pavillon Hotel. For many years, guests and staff have seen the ghosts of an elderly couple in the dining room. The smell of rose perfume has been detected in a room on the third floor. Guests have placed objects in specific places in their rooms before retiring for the night and found that they have been moved to an entirely different spot the next morning. One guest complained that something tried to pull her sheets off her bed at midnight.

Only one of Le Pavillon Hotel's spirits has a name. One of the ghosts is the spirit of a young girl who was run over by a carriage in the 1850s. Folklore identifies her as Eva, Ava and Ada. Some witnesses claim that she asked them for a ride to the ship terminals. Janitors have also seen a man in a dark suit walking along the hallways.

To date, just one guest has been too frightened to spend the entire night in the old hotel. A man who had been attending a medical convention was asleep in his room when he was awakened by the feeling that someone was petting his head. He opened his eyes and was shocked to see an old lady sitting on the side of his bed. After she said, "I will never let you go," he turned on the light, packed his suitcase and checked out of the hotel.

Staff members claim that they receive only one or two reports of ghostly activity each year. The stories bear such a close resemblance to the tales that have been circulating for years that their validity cannot be totally discounted.

St. Bernard Parish

Mercier Plantation

The Mercier Plantation has been owned by members of the Mercier family ever since its construction in St. Bernard Parish in 1831. Over the years, the beautiful old plantation has acquired a reputation for being haunted, primarily because of a legend involving a servant woman's encounter with the ghost of the founder of the plantation years after his death. The following account first appeared in Lyle Saxon's book *Gumbo Ya-Ya* in 1945.

Legend has it that one evening, a black cook named Sarah stepped out of her hot kitchen onto the back porch when she encountered the ghost of Mr. Mercier. In a deep, sonorous voice, he addressed her by name and told her that if she met him behind the milk house at 11:00 p.m., he would reveal to her the location of his buried gold. She was so frightened that she started screaming uncontrollably. Her screams alerted all of the other servants, who ran into the kitchen and asked her what was wrong. After she settled down, the shaken woman told the servants that the ghost of the old master had told her that his gold was buried behind the milk house.

A couple of days passed, and word of the buried treasure on the Mercier planation spread throughout the black community. Gold fever even infected the local preacher, who led a crowd of people to the Mercier plantation. The preacher grabbed a shovel from one of the bystanders and began to dig behind the milk house at 11:00 p.m. Suddenly, the preacher started jumping around and screaming that the devil was attacking him. When he ripped off his shirt, the crowd was shocked to see huge, red welts forming on his back. They also heard the cracking of what sounded like an invisible whip. Sarah, who heard the whipping sound, pushed her way through the crowd and announced that old Master Mercier was punishing the preacher because the ghost wanted her to have the gold. A couple of men picked up the preacher, who was writhing in agony in the mud, and took him home, but the poor man died a few hours later. Mr. Mercier's gold has never been found.

ST. FRANCISVILLE

The Myrtles

General David Bradford built the first part of the Myrtles in 1794 in St. Francisville, Louisiana. Bradford was called "Whiskey Dave" because of his involvement in the Whiskey Rebellion, which got started after the Revolutionary War. The colonists were taxed on corn, sour mash and corn whiskey. Bradford was a prominent attorney in Pennsylvania at this time, and he represented some of the men who grew the corn that made the whiskey. Several hundred farmers banded together under the leadership of Mr. Bradford to protest the taxes. They tarred and feathered tax collectors and burned down one of their houses. By the time the British arrived at Bradford's home in Pennsylvania, he was already gone. He did not want to be imprisoned or hanged, so he fled all the way down to this part of Louisiana. At the time, this area was controlled by the Spanish, so he felt safe from the government. With a Spanish land grant, he bought five hundred acres at $1.40 an acre and built what is now the gift shop. He lived in that building by himself until 1796, when the main part of the house was finished. The old part of the house was known as a "Pennsylvania Saddlebags"–style home, which means that there were four rooms on the ground and four rooms on the upper floor that were accessible only by the outside staircase. Bradford and his wife had several children, but only two of their daughters lived.

Mr. Bradford died in 1808 and left his plantation to his wife, Elizabeth, who ran it for a while. After she died, her daughter, Sarah Matilda, inherited the house and married Judge Clark Woodruff, who was also a successful planter. One day, he was walking through the fields when he noticed a beautiful slave girl named Chloe. He brought her to the house under the pretense of

In 1794, General David Bradford built the first part of the Myrtles plantation house. *Courtesy of the author.*

being a nanny to the children, but she became his mistress as well. Chloe ended up working in the "big house" for seven years. She soon got into the habit of listening to Mr. Woodruff's conversations inside the Gentlemen's Parlor. One evening, while Woodruff was having a business meeting inside the Gentlemen's Parlor, she began listening at the door. Suddenly, the door flew open. Mr. Woodruff not only banished Chloe from the main house, but he also ordered her left ear cut off. From this point on, Chloe always wore a green turban draped down over the left side of her face to conceal her disfigurement.

Chloe wanted to get back in the house because it was better than working out in the hot sun all day long, so she devised a plan to restore herself to the family's good graces. Two of the Woodruff family's three children had birthdays two years and three days apart, so they celebrated their birthdays on the same day. Chloe volunteered to bake the cake for them, but she decided to add an extra ingredient—oleander—which can be commonly found in this part of Louisiana and is extremely poisonous. Chloe's plan was to mix just enough into the birthday cake mix to make the kids sick so she could return to the house and nurse them back to health. She boiled the leaves down and added them to the cake, but unfortunately, two of the children died as a result. When Mr. Woodruff came back from a trip and found out what had happened, he began looking for Chloe, who was hiding in the slave quarters. The slaves didn't want to get themselves into trouble, so they took her back to the main house and made her confess everything to Mr. Woodruff. He ordered that she be hanged from a tree in the back of the plantation by her friends and family. Afterward, they tossed her body into the Mississippi River because they didn't think she deserved a proper burial. Chloe's ghost has been known to tuck people in their beds at night. Also, people standing in the dining room where the little girls ate the poisoned cake have felt someone tugging on the back of their pants or skirts, as if a small child was trying to get their attention. They have also felt coldness in their fingers, as if a small hand had taken hold of theirs.

In 1834, the plantation was sold to the Ruffin Gray Sterling family of Scotland. Sterling increased the acreage to five thousand and bought several hundred more slaves. He planted mostly cotton and indigo. He and his wife had nine children: eight boys and a girl named Sarah. Seven of the boys died in the Civil War. The one who survived—Lewis—was gunned down in the dining room a year later. Just before the Civil War, Sarah married a lawyer named William Winter. The couple had three beautiful children.

The French Room on the first floor was Mrs. Sterling's day room. This is where she came to conduct her business, like giving the servants orders and writing letters. When the house was occupied by a previous owner who was very theatrical, he hired local actors and actresses to portray different characters during the Halloween season. One Halloween, they brought in a young blond high school actress to play the part of Chloe. She was in the bathroom putting on her makeup, and she came into the pitch dark day room with little more than a lit candle in an antique candle holder. She practiced walking around the room, tucking in the children. Suddenly, she saw something in the corner of the room. She said it looked something like a blue shadowy mist. As it approached her, it seemed to be taking the shape of a woman in a ball gown. When the girl took a step forward to get a closer look at the woman's face, her candle went out. She dropped her candle and ran toward the bathroom, but the bathroom door slammed shut before she could run inside, so she lay flat on her back for two and a half minutes, screaming bloody murder. By the time a tour guide on the other side of the house got to her, she had only three things to say:

"Couldn't you have run any faster?"

"I will not be able to play the role of Chloe tonight."

"I swear on my life that I will never contact the Myrtles Plantation again."

Mrs. Sterling is not the only member of the Winter family who has become a ghost. In 1871, William Winter was tutoring his youngest son when a man rode up to the main house and yelled that he needed a lawyer. When William opened the door, he was shot. Clutching his chest, William staggered up to the seventeenth step of the main staircase, where he collapsed and died in Sarah's arms. Ever since his murder, heavy, labored steps have been heard climbing the steps of the main staircase, stopping on the seventeenth step.

After her husband's death, Sarah became a total recluse. She locked herself in the room at the top of the stairs for several months. She eventually starved herself to death. People spending the night in this room have heard footsteps trudging up to the seventeenth step late in the evening. They have also heard faint sobbing in one of the corners of the room.

The mirror in the lower foyer is quite possibly the most famous haunted mirror in the United States. Whenever someone in the family died in the eighteenth and nineteenth centuries, his or her body would be brought to

The spectral sobbing of Sarah Winter has been heard in a corner of her room at the top of the main staircase. *Courtesy of the author.*

the house for viewing. The mourners always made sure to cover every single mirror with a thick black cloth. They feared that the soul of the deceased person might rise up, see its reflection in the mirror and become trapped in it. The staff believes that this is what happened to this mirror. People have made out the image of a face in the glass. Down the left side of the mirror is a child-like fingerprint coming down from the top. The truly interesting thing about these marks on the mirror is that none of them can be removed. The mirror has been taken apart and refiltered on at least ten different occasions. Every time this is done, the exact same marks reappear in the exact same places within the space of a week. This is the one part of the tour where guests are allowed to take pictures. Sometimes things appear in guests' pictures that weren't in the mirror when they took them. Some people think that the ghosts of Sarah and her two daughters are trapped here.

The John W. Leake Room is haunted by the ghost of a Confederate officer who came here to heal from a leg injury that he had received in battle. Sarah and her servants cared for him as best they could. After a few days, however, he developed gangrene. His leg had to be amputated, and he died in that room. This is the only room where the staff has gotten reports of physical pain from people who have stayed here. Several guests have been awakened in the middle of the night by a sharp, stabbing pain in their left leg, the same leg that Mr. Leake had amputated. A few guests have also been awakened by the overwhelming smell of cigar smoke, as if someone was blowing smoke in their faces. As it turns out, Mr. Leake was an avid cigar smoker. Guests have also walked into this room and found a Confederate officer's uniform lying on the bed or hanging in the closet. They usually come downstairs and tell the staff that a reenactor has left his things there. Actually, reenactors never stay at the Myrtles. The staff thinks that Mr. Leake makes his presence known in this room because it is his way of saying that it is and always will be his room.

I have always been intrigued by the history and mystery of the Myrtles, which the Smithsonian has deemed the most haunted house in the United States. My wife, Marilyn, and I celebrated our thirty-sixth wedding anniversary at the Myrtles on June 14 and 15, 2012. Actually, she didn't tell me that we were going there. I figured it out when she said she had booked us a weekend at a place I had always wanted to visit.

My wife and I spent the night in the William Winter Room. There are not a lot of amenities here. There is no television. The four-poster bed was pretty hard, and it was so high off the floor that my wife had to use her suitcase like a step. The walls were very thin, so we heard every sound the people made in the next room. A sign in the room advised people not to eat in the rooms. When I heard the owner, Tia Moss, talking to an exterminator on the phone about the "mice problems," I realized why. The noises in the house made it almost impossible to record EVPs, although we did try.

However, we did capture some visual evidence. Whenever I visit a haunted bed-and-breakfast, I like to take a few pictures before we unpack our suitcases. One of the first photos I took was of a chair. When I examined the photo, I noticed that that my wife's image was in the mirror. I asked her to step aside, and a few seconds later, I took another photo. The orb that is clearly visible on the chair could be connected to one of the ghost stories about this room. In 1867, William Winter lost one of his daughters to yellow fever. Then another lovely daughter, Katie, contracted the disease about two months later in January 1868. He spent a lot of money trying to cure her, but nothing seemed to work. In desperation, his wife, Sarah, begged her handmaid to get a voodoo queen named Cleo from a neighboring plantation to see if she could cure the girl. The woman spent all night in this room chanting and performing rituals while Mr. Winter paced around the bottom floor of his house, wishing and praying that his daughter would be healed. Just before sunrise, Cleo walked down the stairs and told William that Katie was resting peacefully and that she would recover. He ran up to his daughter's bedside and waited for his daughter to wake up.

She never did. Mr. Winter was so enraged that he took his anger out on Cleo. That night, Cleo was dragged out of the house and lynched from a tree. Cleo's ghost has been seen walking around the edges of the plantation. People staying in the William Winter Room have heard a very quiet chanting. One night, a lady sleeping in the room was awakened by a creaking noise. When she awoke, she saw a woman hanging from a chandelier directly above her bed. She pulled the covers over her face and did not raise them up until the creaking noise dissipated. The shadowy figure of Cleo has also appeared dancing across the walls and peering over people who are sleeping in the room.

It turns out that almost all of the people who were staying at the Myrtles that night on our anniversary trip were just like us—over fifty and interested in the ghost stories. A woman and her daughter who stayed in the Julia Leake Room across the hall from us said that they left their luggage inside the room at 2:30 p.m. on June 14. At 2:45 p.m., before they left, they took pictures of the cooler and other objects they had strategically placed in the room. When they returned thirty minutes later, they checked out the objects they had placed around the room. Everything was just as they had left it.

Left: An orb is clearly visible on this chair in the William Winter Room, where one of Winter's daughters died of yellow fever. *Courtesy of the author.*

Below: A woman sleeping in the William Winter Room saw the ghost of a woman hanging from the ceiling above her. *Courtesy of the author.*

However, when the woman looked back at the entrance to the room, she screamed because the blue cooler was now sitting outside the bathroom door. It had previously been sitting inside the room. Also, the toilet paper roll, which she had changed so it would unroll from the top, had been put back in its original position (unrolling from the bottom).

On June 14, 2012, one of the ladies who worker at the Myrtles was cleaning the rooms in the main house. She'd been working for about an hour when she noticed that one of the pearl earrings her daughter had given her was no longer on her ear. She looked in all the rooms she'd just cleaned, but no trace of the earring could be found. She didn't understand how the earring could have fallen off her ear because it locked on. She hoped it would turn up because of its sentimental value.

On the night of June 15, a lady who had just taken the Friday night ghost tour with her husband put her two earrings on top of the mantel and went to sleep. The next morning, she walked over to the mantel and discovered that one of her earrings was gone. She searched all over and was surprised to find the missing earring clear across the room on the dresser. Staff members say that Chloe is probably the culprit because she seems to like earrings.

A guest who had placed her earrings on the mantle in this bedroom was surprised that one of them had been moved across the room to a dresser during the night. *Courtesy of the author.*

The apparition of a nude Indian woman has been seen inside this gazebo. *Courtesy of the author.*

That same night, the woman's husband was taking pictures on the grounds. At 11:00 p.m., he took several photos of the gazebo on the small island in the middle of the pond. When he looked at the photos later, there were mists in the gazebo in two of the photos. The ghost of a naked Indian maiden has been known to stand inside the gazebo.

Is the Myrtles haunted? The things my wife and I experienced that weekend and the things that the other guests experienced would suggest to me that it is. The Myrtles is like Disneyworld for ghost hunters.

SUNSET

Chretien Point Plantation

In the early 1800s, Hypolite Chretien owned a cotton plantation in Opelousas, Louisiana. Legend has it that in January 1815 during the Battle of New Orleans, Hypolite was crouched down in a ditch with his uncle when a young man ran in front of them. Suddenly, the man fell down, struck in the leg with a British bullet. Hypolite grabbed the young man and pulled him to safety. The young man thanked Hypolite profusely and introduced himself as Jean Lafitte.

After the battle, Hypolite returned to his cotton plantation in Opelousas, and Jean Lafitte resumed his life as a pirate. A few years later, Lafitte realized that he could profit from his friendship with the Canadian cotton planter. One day, Lafitte visited Hypolite's planation in Opelousas Point. Settling in a chair with a glass of brandy in his hand, Lafitte proposed that Hypolite allow Lafitte to use the land he owned in Chretien Point as the base of his smuggling operation. Hypolite viewed his friend's scheme as a way of making him and his new wife rich. Using the wealth they had acquired through the buying and selling of contraband goods and undocumented slaves, Hypolite and his wife, Felicite, built a magnificent plantation home between 1831 and 1835 as the centerpiece of their 640-acre cotton plantation at Chretien Point near Sunset, Louisiana. The plantation house was clearly constructed with Louisiana's hot, humid weather in mind. All of the main rooms opened onto the upper and lower galleries, thereby allowing cool breezes to waft through the house. Copies of the distinctive ramp knee staircase and fan light windows are said to have been used in the movie *Gone with the Wind*.

After Hypolite succumbed to a bout of yellow fever, Felicite became the mistress of Chretien Point Plantation. Felicite was a strong woman who was perfectly capable of managing the large plantation and its five hundred slaves on her own. Supposedly, she dug up the gold Hypolite had buried and, through shrewd business deals, doubled his savings. Her neighbors viewed her as eccentric because of her habit of smoking cigars and playing cards. Not long after Hypolite's death, the remaining members of Lafitte's band of pirates, with whom Felecite was still doing business, decided to leave their hideout in Galveston and rob the grieving widow of Chretien Point Plantation. The story goes that late one night, Felicite was putting her children to bed when she heard movement in the front yard. She looked out the window and gasped when she saw a group of men creeping stealthily up the front walk. Grabbing a pistol, she made her way to the front stairs, just as the pirates forced open the front door. The leader of the pirates asked Felicite where she kept her jewels and gold. She replied, "In one of the bedrooms upstairs." As the pirate proceeded to climb the stairs, she pulled out the pistol she had hidden behind her back and shot the pirate in the forehead. He collapsed in a heap on the eleventh stair. As the other pirates ran back down the stairs, Felicite then yelled for her servants to come quickly to the main entrance of the house. She distributed rifles and pistols to all of the servants and drove away the pirates. After they had fled, Felticite ordered the servants to bury the pirate's corpse in an unmarked grave on the grounds, where he remains to this day.

Chretien Point Plantation suffered considerable damage during the Civil War. In 1863, the Battle of Little Crow Bayou was waged on the plantation grounds. During the battle, a Union cannonball destroyed parts of the roof and the upper section of the westernmost column of the house. A stray bullet is still embedded in one of the front doors. Felicite's son, Hypolite II, saved the plantation from total destruction by raising a Masonic flag. It turned out that the commander of the Union forces was also a Mason, and he ordered his men to cease fire. Felicite gave rations to the hungry Union soldiers and ordered her servants to bury the Confederate dead in a mass grave.

The old plantation house stood abandoned during much of the twentieth century. In her book *The Haunting of Louisiana*, author Barbara Sillery says that when the present owners, Louis and Jeanne Cornay, purchased the property in 1975, the old mansion was in terrible disrepair. Farmers had been storing hay and keeping animals inside the once-beautiful plantation home. As the Cornays were remodeling the interior of the house, they noticed a dark stain on the eleventh stair of the staircase. No amount of scrubbing would remove it. When the Cornays heard the legend of the death of the pirate on the staircase, they decided to leave the stain alone.

Today, Chretien Point Plantation is run as an inn, the main attraction of which seems to be the ghosts that roam its halls and grounds. One of these ghosts is the spirit of Felicite Chretien, who appears on the second floor wearing a wide-brimmed hat and black netting extending down to her waist. Many people driving by the plantation have seen her staring out of one of the windows in the Magnolia Room, holding back the curtains. The ghosts of companies of soldiers killed during the Battle of Little Crow Bayou are still marching in formation across the grounds late in the evening. The loud clomping of heavy boots has been heard on the staircase where the pirate died and in the parlor and dining area. The ghost of a female cousin who drowned in the bayou has been seen walking across the grounds. In the late 1960s, the son of one of the owners was walking around the backyard of the plantation with a friend when they saw a Civil War soldier with one leg perched in a tree. In 2006, a wedding that was held at the plantation was disrupted by a bizarre knocking sound coming from an armoire. The guests opened the door and found nothing inside. The identity of this particular spirit has not been discovered.

Like the owners of many haunted inns in the South, Louis and Jeanne Cornay have decided to celebrate the ghosts in their establishment. Once a month, the Cornays throw a ghost dinner that includes a guided ghost tour of the plantation. It is said that very few of the guests are disappointed by the food—or the ghosts.

Mississippi

Bay St. Louis

Hancock County Courthouse

The first county seat in Hancock County was Center, which later changed its name to Caesar to avoid confusion with another town in Mississippi named Center. The first courthouse was a log building that was erected in 1817 after Mississippi was admitted into the Union. When the population of the county shifted, the county seat was moved several times until it finally ended up in Shieldsboro—now known as Bay St. Louis—in 1857. The basement of the newly erected city hall served as the first courthouse. As the size of the county increased, a new courthouse building was necessary. The grand wooden structure was completed at a cost of $6,000 in 1874 on the site of the present courthouse. By 1910, the county had decided to build another new courthouse. The board of supervisors accepted a bid for the construction of the courthouse at 150 Main Street on September 20, 1911. The courthouse has weathered the effects of time for over a century, including Hurricane Camille. The courthouse also endured the blasts of Hurricane Katrina in 2005 but had to be extensively repaired afterward. Today, the Hancock County Courthouse has been lovingly restored. According to testimony from witnesses, though, the structural changes might have awakened several spirits from Hancock County's past.

A considerable amount of paranormal activity has occurred at the courthouse over the years. The most commonly sighted spirit is a ghostly woman in white who has been seen many times on the staircase in the lobby. In 2012, a policeman who was working late in the building saw a woman he described as "transparent" walking up the staircase. He ran up the staircase and followed her down a hallway, but he lost her when she rounded a corner. Women walking through the building have heard a female voice calling their name. This spirit is thought to be the widow of a man who was hanged in the early 1900s. Many policemen have heard footsteps on the second floor late at night when the building was supposed to be empty, and several policemen have heard water running in the shower area, even though the water is turned off. Some people have heard doors slamming in the middle of the night. A policeman who has worked in the courthouse for many years has heard spectral laughter and voices late at night. Another policeman was in the courtroom when he saw a shadowy figure standing in the back by the doors.

On August 18, 2012, the Central Mississippi Paranormal Society conducted a formal investigation of the Hancock County Courthouse. During the night, members saw a shadowy figure standing in front of a window. The leader of the group, Trent Lewis, said that the figure blocked out the glare of the street lamp shining through the window. One member saw balls of light in one of the hallways. Trent was standing in the courtroom when he saw a shadow figure peeking through the doorway. The investigators left the courthouse convinced that there might be some truth to the stories that have been circulating around town for many years.

BILOXI

The Old Biloxi Regional Hospital

Construction of the Old Biloxi Regional Hospital began in the late 1920s. The hospital was dedicated on July 3, 1929. In 1963, the hospital became the New Biloxi Hospital. After a few years, the old hospital changed its mission entirely and became the Gulf Coast Convalescent Center. After the Gulf Coast Convalescent Center closed on October 31, 1979, it remained vacant until October 1984, when it was reopened as the Biloxi Regional Outreach

Center, where patients were treated for substance abuse. Two years later, the hospital was renamed the Bienville Recovery Center after it was leased to South Mississippi Health Services.

By 1996, the old hospital stood abandoned. Graffiti covered the walls; broken glass and pieces of discarded equipment littered the hallways. The only visitors were transients and teenagers. In 1996, the east service wing was heavily damaged by fire. In 2004, the State of Mississippi renovated the hospital for use as a state building at a cost of $8 million. Today, few people who get their driver's licenses at the modern-looking building would guess that at one time it was a haunted hospital.

The building first gained a reputation as a haunted place in the 1930s. Medical personnel and patients reported that doors opened and shut by themselves. Some people walking down the hallways late at night said that they passed through what can best be described as cold spots. White, wispy figures were seen walking down the hallway. A number of terminally ill patients complained to the nurses that they were being annoyed by two little girls who stood at the foot of their beds. All of the patients died soon after seeing the little girls, leading some staff members to believe that they were acting as guides to the "other side." After the building was closed, the police were called to the abandoned building to investigate the sound of someone screaming inside the old hospital. While they were walking down the hallway, they heard several high-pitched screams and the whimpering of a little girl. They also heard the rattling of old-fashioned iron beds. They checked out every room but were unable to find anyone else inside the building. Thrill-seeking teenagers swore that they heard the sounds of a baby crying and phantom conversations inside the building. Now that the building is no longer a hospital, the ghost stories have become nothing more than a fading memory.

Beauvoir

Beauvoir was the last home Jefferson Davis ever owned. It was built in 1848 by a wealthy planter named James Brown as a summer home for his family. The house was originally called Orange Grove because of the satsuma orange trees that grew in abundance on the property. The eight-room house is a raised cottage, resting on massive brick pillars that allow floodwaters to flow through the ground level of the house. Brown tried to take advantage of the Gulf's cool sea breeze by incorporating wide porches, high ceilings and

Beauvoir was the last home owned by Jefferson Davis. *Courtesy of the author.*

large windows into his building plan. Brown also constructed two smaller cottages in the front yard and several outbuildings in the back, such as the kitchen. Following Brown's death in 1857, his widow sold the house to a real estate speculator.

In 1873, a wealthy author named Sarah Ellis Dorsey became the next owner of the house that she promptly renamed Beauvoir. Over the next few years, she became known locally for her lavish parties. In 1977, Sarah received a visit from a family friend, Jefferson Davis, who was looking for a quiet place to write. For the next two years, he rented one of the two smaller cottages in the front yard for $50 per month. By 1879, Davis had decided that he wanted to purchase Beauvoir. He agreed to pay Mrs. Dorsey three installments of $5,500. Davis made the first payment; six months later, Mrs. Dorsey died and willed Beauvoir to Davis, who moved in with his wife, Varina, and their youngest daughter, Winnie.

After completing *Short History of the Confederate States of America*, Davis made an excursion to Brierfield Plantation near Vicksburg. Davis contracted a life-threatening fever during the trip and had to be transported to New Orleans for treatment. On December 6, 1889, Davis died of bronchitis complicated by malaria. In his will, Davis left Beauvoir to Winnie. In 1891, Varina and Winnie moved to New York City.

After Winnie died in 1898, Varina took possession of the plantation house. In 1902, Varina sold her husband's retirement home to the Sons of

Confederate Veterans for $10,000. She intended for the house to stand as a shrine to her late husband. To accommodate the 2,500 Confederate veterans and their widows, the Sons of Confederate Veterans constructed a hospital, a chapel and a dozen barracks. In 1941, Beauvoir became a tour home. In 1957, the Confederate Veterans Home closed after the last three Confederate widows were moved to a nursing home in Greenwood, Mississippi.

Beauvoir continues to be owned and operated by the Mississippi Branch of the Sons of Confederate Veterans. The lovely old home has withstood the ravages of both time and nature. In 1969, Beauvoir was flooded in the aftermath of Hurricane Camille but, for the most part, avoided any really serious damage. However, the damage inflicted on Beauvoir by Hurricane Katrina in 2005 was much more severe. Even though the six brick fireplaces reinforced the outside walls and prevented them from collapsing, the hurricane destroyed the home's roof and its newly restored porches. Because Beauvoir is a U.S. National Historic Landmark, repairs were funded with federal monies. The restoration of Beauvoir began in 2006 and ended in 2008.

Jefferson Davis is buried at Hollywood Cemetery in Richmond, Virginia, but his spirit appears to have remained in his beloved home. In Sylvia Booth Hubbard's book *Ghosts! Personal Accounts of Modern Mississippi Hauntings*, the former superintendent of Beauvoir, Colonel Newton Carr Jr., said that a hostess reported seeing tears streaming down the cheeks of one of the busts. A large number of people have caught fleeting glimpses of the ghosts of both Jefferson Davis and his wife. People have also seen the spectral figure of a tall man wearing a top hat and a frock coat walking through the rose garden late at night. Other ghosts appear to be inhabiting Beauvoir as well. Several of the guards swore that they saw the ghosts of some of the old Confederate veterans walking around the house. Colonel Carr himself encountered a cold spot on the property. "I'd be walking on the grounds on a hot summer afternoon and get a chill by walking through a cold area," Carr said. The former superintendent also heard a loud crashing noise early one morning while watching television. Carr said that it sounded as if several bookshelves had fallen down. He walked through the entire house but was unable to find anything out of order. Later, Carr discovered that guests sleeping in the house had heard the same sound.

In the twenty-first century, the spirits of Beauvoir began showing up in photographs. In 2003, Angie, one of the tour guides, was having her photograph taken outside of the house. Behind her in one of the lower windows, one can see a couple dressed in period antebellum clothing. No one else was in the house at the time. In 2008, more photographic evidence surfaced supporting the rumors that Beauvoir is haunted. A guest who was

The apparition of a tall man resembling this statue of Jefferson Davis has been sighted walking the grounds of Beauvoir. *Courtesy of the author.*

touring Beauvoir caught a startling image in Winnie Davis's bedroom. In the photograph, one can clearly see a swirling mist, about the size of a human being, hovering over the bed. The mist was not visible to the naked eye.

The resurrection of Beauvoir in the years following Hurricane Katrina's visit to Biloxi is even more miraculous when one views the photographs documenting the damage. The surging water washed priceless antiques through the first floor of the house and piled them against the walls. A piano was discovered at the top of a tree. Of the collections housed in Beauvoir, 60 percent were salvaged, an amazing number considering the ferocity of the storm. One could argue that the durability of this mid-nineteenth-century building reflects the endurance of the Davis family, whose spirits seem to have survived death itself.

Deer Island

Deer Island, which was once part of the mainland, is the closest island to the Mississippi Gulf Coast. The 674-acre island lies in the Gulf of Mexico, just southeast of Biloxi, Mississippi. It was designated a Mississippi Coastal Preserve in 2002. The terrain consists of salt marshes, salt grasses, pine trees and white beaches. American alligators, ospreys, mottled ducks, loggerhead turtles and diamondback turtles all inhabit Deer Island. A number of rare or endangered species also live there, including oystercatchers, least terns, snowy plover, piping plovers, brown pelicans, American kestrels and sharp-shinned hawks. Rarer still is an unearthly presence that, according to legend, can also be found on Deer Island.

The story goes that in the eighteenth century, the captain of a pirate ship selected Deer Island as the place where he would bury a chest of ill-gotten gold. The crew waited on the ship, anchored just off Deer Island, while the captain and his landing party rowed to shore. After the men disembarked, they dug a deep pit in a secluded spot and buried the chest. While the pirates lowered the chest into the hole in the ground, the captain asked if anyone would volunteer to stand guard over the buried treasure for a while. The only one who raised his hand was a young man who had just joined the pirate crew and was anxious to prove himself. Smiling broadly, the captain put his hand on the pirate's shoulder and thanked him for his dedication. A few seconds later, before the young man knew what was happening, the captain drew his cutlass and lopped off the pirate's head. The captain then ordered his men to dump the young man's corpse into the treasure pit and cover it up so that his spirit would become a ghostly guardian of pirate gold.

Many years later, three fishermen who had been trolling in the Gulf decided to beach their boat on Deer Island and spend the night there. They pitched their tent and built a fire. After they had finished dining on some of the fish they had caught, the men lay down in the sand, taking in the cool sea breezes. They were looking forward to showing their fine catch to their friends and families. Suddenly, the stillness was broken by the sound of shuffling feet. The men sat up, fully expecting to see a wild hog charging at them from the palmettos. Their blood ran cold when, in the flickering light of their campfire, they beheld a headless skeleton staggering out of the trees in their direction. Screaming, the men got up and ran back to the boat, where they spent the night. The next morning, the men returned to their campsite to retrieve their tent and utensils. Turning their heads in every direction, they cautiously made their way back to the tent, fully expecting to see the skeletal interloper. They were relieved to find that they were the only people—living or dead—on the island.

If Deer Island had not been declared a Gulf Ecological Management Site, it would be dotted with casinos. When one takes into consideration the headless guardian's disdain for treasure hunters of any sort, it is probably just as well that gamblers eager to "strike it rich" will not be doing so on Deer Island.

Mary Mahoney's

Mary Mahoney's, one of the finest restaurants in Mississippi, is located in the oldest house in Biloxi. The land on which the main house was built was part of a

Mary Mahoney suspected that her restaurant was haunted when it first opened its doors in 1962. *Courtesy of the author.*

land grant to Louis Frasier, who moved to Biloxi in 1729. The four-room house was constructed of hand-made brick and hand-hewn cypress, and oak boards of various widths were used for the floor. The second floor was a single great room, which had a large fireplace. From the windows on the second floor, one could see the walled courtyard and a huge live oak tree, which is estimated to be over two thousand years old. The slate roof was imported from France. Slabs of slate were also used to cover the floor of the porch. The old French House, as it was known for many years, was one of the few homes in the area with a cellar. The slave quarters and the kitchen were detached from the main house.

Frasier's descendants continued living in the house until 1820. People of various nationalities owned the house until 1962, when the new owners—Mary Mahoney; her husband, Bob; and her brother, Andrew Cvitanovich—decided to convert the old residence into a restaurant. During the remodeling process, which took two years, the Mahoneys took great care to preserve the original flooring, brickwork and fireplaces. An architect from Vicksburg, Jack Canizaro, suggested that the slave quarters be connected to the main house and that two small dining rooms be added as well. While Andrew directed the restoration of the house, Mary set about buying tables from the Salvation Army and Goodwill.

She procured other furnishings, like lamps, from flea markets. The silver, pots and pans came from an auction at the old Miramar Hotel. Mary Mahoney's finally opened for business in 1964. The old building was restored once again in 2005 after Hurricane Katrina. The twenty-eight-foot storm surge severely damaged the dining rooms and kitchen. The heart pine floors, which were buckled by the water that filled the first floor, had to be replaced for the first time since the 1700s. However, the walls were still structurally sound, and the restaurant was open for business once again after only nine weeks.

A member of the Lord of the Dance troupe saw a shadowy figure walk through the doors of the men's restroom. *Courtesy of the author.*

Mary Mahoney began to suspect that the Old French House was haunted soon after the restaurant opened its doors. Eileen, Mary Mahoney's daughter, said that her mother and father were sitting in the kitchen after hours one day when suddenly all the pots and pans fell off the hooks. Over the years, eyewitness accounts from guests confirmed Mary's suspicions that she was sharing the building with spirits. "Several years ago, there was a psychic who was performing over at the Hard Rock Casino across the street," Eileen said. "He was sitting in this addition to the restaurant, and one of the servers asked him how his meal was. He said, 'The redcoats in this room are so thick that I can't even eat. They're running back and forth across the room.' And then he went in the attic, and he went in the cellar, and he said he was going to come back because he was sensing all kinds of things, but he never did."

Shortly before Hurricane Katrina struck Biloxi, the cast of Lord of the Dance had an otherworldly experience at Mary Mahoney's. "We were just having fun with them," Eileen said. "In front of the men's room where the receptionist stands was a big old hall tree with a mirror. One of them said, 'Something just walked into that bathroom. It was like a shadow.' Of course, we checked it out, and there was no one in there. When we told him that we couldn't find anyone, he said, 'I swear that somebody just walked by me.'"

The servers believe that the second floor is haunted by the ghost of Angelique, the wife of a sailor who lived in the house. Apparently, her bedroom was on the second floor. Strange noises, like bumps and disembodied footsteps, have been reported in the restaurant, usually after closing.

The existence of ghosts in Mary Mahoney's will be difficult, if not impossible, to prove. There is no doubt, though, that for believers in the paranormal, the history and lore of the old restaurant enhance the dining experience.

GAUTIER

Great Hope Cemetery

Gautier, a city in Jackson County, is located on the West Bank of the Pascagoula River, also known as the "Singing River." After the Civil War, Fernando Upton Gautier, for whom the city is named, and his wife, Theresa Bayard Gautier, from New Orleans, built a home on the West Bank. Descendants of the Gautier family still live in the family mansion, known today as the "Old Place." After Gautier's sawmill was fully operational, a number of families began moving into the area. Before long, trains began stopping at the burgeoning town to pick up the lumber produced at Gautier's sawmill.

Gautier remained a small town until World War II, when ships were built at Bob Ingalls's shipyard to support the war effort. The population of Gautier experienced a growth spurt when the shipyard workers brought their families with them. In the 1960s, the population of Gautier increased once again when the shipyard was expanded by the new owners, Litton Industries. Gautier, which was incorporated in 1986, is now one of the fifty largest cities in Mississippi. Even though Gautier's rural ambience has diminished over the years, a few reminders of the past are still in evidence. A number of the old homes, such as the Portas Homestead and Oldfields, are still standing. One of the city's most intriguing historical sites, Garden of Hope Cemetery, has been named one of the top ten haunted cemeteries in the United States.

The cemetery's best-known ghost story dates back to the late 1970s. A man named Hal who had traveled to Gautier to work in the shipyard invited his wife, Susan, and his children to stay at a local hotel so that they could begin looking for the house they were going to purchase with his bonus money. On the day his family was scheduled to arrive in Gautier, the man's vision of his dream house went up in smoke when he received word that he was being laid off. On the way to the hotel, the desperate man's fevered brain concocted a crazy scheme to prevent his family from being devastated by the bad news. When Hal entered the family's hotel room, he pretended that everything was all right. He told them that the next morning they would all look at the house he was planning to buy. That night, while his family was asleep, Hal walked out of the hotel and returned a few minutes later with a fire ax. He then proceeded to murder his wife and five children as they lay asleep in their bed. After he had killed the last of their five children, he staggered out into the rain with a glazed look in his eyes. As he crossed the highway, he was struck and killed by a truck that, ironically, was transporting a propeller for the ship he had just gotten fired from. The entire family was buried in Garden of Hope of Cemetery. For decades, people have seen children frolicking among the tombstones. The ghostly figure of the homicidal father roams the cemetery as well, searching for his children.

One of Hal and Susan's children seems to enjoy mingling with visitors to Garden of Hope Cemetery. The ghost of a little girl between ten and twelve years old is said to walk up to people and introduce herself. She then follows visitors around the cemetery, helping them look for a particular grave. At times, she even offers to hold the flowers they are carrying. Witnesses say that just before they leave the graveyard, the little girl vanishes before their eyes. A paranormal group investigating the cemetery recorded an EVP of a little girl saying, "Hope you'll come back to see me soon."

An older—and much more sinister—female ghost also haunts Garden of Hope Cemetery. The ghost, who is known as "Bloody Sarah," is described as a middle-aged woman with red hair who wears a bloody housecoat and fluffy white bedroom slippers. She seems to enjoy terrifying people driving past the cemetery by running in front of their cars. Thinking that they have run over an actual human being, the drivers usually stop to look for the person they think they have killed. As they walk along the road, they hear the maniacal laughter of a woman.

An even more frightening female spirit is the ghost of a woman known only as Joanna. The story goes that late one night, Joanna followed her husband to the middle of Garden of Hope Cemetery, where he and his lover were locked in an amorous embrace. She raised the pistol she had brought and shot both of them, killing them instantly. She then walked up to the cemetery gate, put the gun to her head and pulled the trigger. People who have trespassed inside the cemetery late at night claim that they have been chased and even struck by Joanna's vengeful apparition.

A larcenous spirit also haunts Garden of Hope Cemetery. The spirit of a man whose grave never receives visitors is said to rise from his grave at night and steal the flowers from nearby graves. The missing flowers always appear on his grave the next day. His most famous manifestation occurred late one dark afternoon when a woman who was a member of a funeral party was approached by a strange-looking man who grabbed the bouquet she was holding and ran off. The other mourners found the flowers on top of another grave after the funeral. The woman recognized the photograph on his tombstone as the image of the man who had accosted her.

Even a gravedigger who was employed at the cemetery has returned as a spirit to Garden of Hope Cemetery. In 1965, the gravedigger, known only as Gus, was walking down the highway toward his home at 5:00 p.m. when he was hit and killed by a car. Since then, he has been walking through the gates at quitting time and walking down the highway. Gus's spirit has also been picked up by drivers while walking home. As Gus and the car or truck driver pass the cemetery, he says, "This is where I died." The apparition then dissolves into nothingness. Witnesses describe Gus as being a friendly man who has dirt on his hands and knees.

Like many towns and cities located on the Gulf Coast, Gautier suffered a direct hit from Hurricane Katrina on August 29, 2005. A number of the city's homes were destroyed in the storm. Garden of Hope Cemetery and its resident spirits, however, are still around.

OCEAN SPRINGS

Rock and Roll Cemetery

The William Seymour Memorial Cemetery is located two miles northeast of Ocean Springs on the west side of Bayou Talla. On April 8, 1856, the State of Mississippi patented this tract of land to Peter Seymour. Following Peter's death, William Seymour acquired the land on September 22, 1888. However, in 1902, William forfeited the land for his failure to pay the taxes. Mrs. M.V. Russell purchased the land for $7.50, but her husband, Hiram Fisher Russell, sold one acre back to the Seymour family to be used exclusively as a family cemetery. Today, the William Seymour Memorial Cemetery is still an active burial ground. The passing of time has taken its toll on the little graveyard, though. It has been heavily vandalized over the years because it is surrounded by woods and, therefore, has become a favorite hangout for teenagers, who believe it is haunted.

No one knows for certain how the William Seymour Memorial Cemetery acquired the name "Rock and Roll Cemetery." Older residents of Ocean Springs can recall back in the 1950s when teenagers drove their dates to the out-of-the-way spot and played rock-and-roll music on their car radios. According to one legend, which bears a very strong resemblance to a popular urban legend, a young couple drove out to the old graveyard after the prom in the 1950s and parked under a large tree. While they were "necking," they heard a noise out in the woods. The boy told his date that he was going to see who was out there and instructed her not to unlock the car door unless he knocked three times. Twenty minutes later, she heard two knocks but fell asleep while waiting for the third. When she awoke the next morning, she climbed out of the car and screamed when she saw her boyfriend's body hanging from the tree. The murderer was said to be a member of a family of albinos who enjoyed killing young people who trespassed at the cemetery late at night.

Stories of graveyard ghosts have also been generated around the old cemetery. One popular story has to do with the ghost of an old lady who has been seen sitting in a rocking chair. When she notices people watching her, she leaps from her chair and chases them out of the graveyard. A few boys have even claimed to have found the decrepit rocking chair in the woods. According to another commonly told tale, people riding through the cemetery notice that the road had fourteen curves when they drove in but thirteen curves when they left. Reports of weird sounds—cries, moans, growls and screams—are also commonplace. Photographs of a tree from which a man is said to have hanged himself have revealed an eerie glow around the limb where the rope was tied. Some teenagers swear that some invisible force pushed them off the tombstones they sit on.

The truth is that most—if not all—of these stories are apocryphal. As of this printing, very little evidence beyond personal experiences has been collected proving that the William Seymour Memorial Cemetery is haunted. Members of the group Chicago Paranormal Investigators recorded no EMFs (electronic magnetic fields), no EVPs and no extreme fluctuations in temperature during their nighttime visit to the old cemetery. A daytime investigation conducted by the Ozarks Paranormal Society yielded similar results. A few orbs have been photographed here, but they are most likely nothing more than bugs. Visitors should remember that this is not an abandoned cemetery, despite its remote location. Generations of the Seymour family have been—and will continue to be—interred here. To them, this is a sacred place, not a hotbed of paranormal activity. Curiosity seekers should respect the families' desire for privacy. They should also be aware that the graveyard is closed at night and that trespassers will be prosecuted.

MERIDIAN

The Old Lauderdale County Jail

The first Lauderdale County Courthouse was built in 1890. After it burned down in 1903, a new courthouse was built on the same site between 1904 and 1905. The building underwent a number of architectural changes in 1939 as part of the Federal Works Project. Not only was the entire building enlarged and remodeled in the Art Deco style, but the courthouse dome was also removed, and a new jail was built on top of the courthouse. In the early 1990s, it became clear that the jail, which was showing its age, was too small. The jail was closed in July 1998. The date was Friday the Thirteenth.

Rumors that the old jail was haunted have attracted the attention of a number of paranormal investigators over the year. In December 2011, a local group of paranormal investigators, Ghost Chasers of Mississippi, spent the night in the old jail. This writer, along with director Justin Pritchett and a young member of the group, walked into one of the cells in the women's section of the jail. I sat on a bunk and set a flashlight next to me. I then addressed the spirit inside the jail: "We would like to make contact with you. If the answer to my question is 'Yes,' please signify by flashing the light once. If the is answer is 'No,' please signify by flashing twice."

I asked a series of questions but received no response. I then asked the young man in the group to sit on the bunk and continued with my questions. When I asked, "Do you think this young man is handsome?" the flashlight flashed once. When I asked "Do you like this guy?" the flashlight flashed once. When I asked, "Would you like to go home with this young man?" the flashlight flashed once again. By this time, the young man had become uneasy and left the cells.

I returned to the old jail once again on October 29, 2012, with Paula Merritt, a photographer for the *Meridian Star*; Steve Thomas, policeman with the Meridian Police Department; and three other policemen, one of whom, Deputy Chris Swanner of the Lauderdale County School District, worked at the jail before it closed. He even cut down one of several prisoners who

The old Lauderdale County Jail was erected on top of the Lauderdale County Courthouse in 1939. *Courtesy of the author.*

Paula Merritt, a photographer for the *Meridian Star*, is seen taking EMF readings inside the old Lauderdale County Jail. *Courtesy of the author.*

A jail cell where a prisoner hanged himself years ago. *Courtesy of the author.*

had committed suicide inside the jail. As we walked through the jail, several members of the group said that shadowy forms were moving between the cells. An hour later, we were standing outside of the elevator next to the women's section when all of us heard a very faint female voice. No members of the group were speaking at the time.

The strangest event took place when we were standing in a small section of the jail where a prisoner had hanged himself. Paula and I sat inside the cell while the others stood in the hall. I set the flashlight on the bench and asked the spirit to flash once for "Yes" and twice for "No." I asked the spirit if he was at rest. No response. I then asked if he deserved to be in jail. No response. This pattern continued until I asked, "Did you like the guards?" The flashlight flashed twice. I then asked, "Were the guards mean to you?" The flashlight flashed twice. The session ended when I asked, "Do you wish you could leave?" The flashlight flashed once. The spirit was finished, and so were we.

Natchez

The Burn

The Burn was built in 1834 by John Walworth. *Burn* is a Scottish word for "brook." A drawing showing how the home looked in 1834 is on display in the front hall. Walworth's family lived in the Greek Revival home for one hundred years, with the exception of a three-year period during the Civil War when it served as the headquarters of Major Jon P. Coleman. Coleman's name, carved with a diamond, is clearly visible in one of the windowpanes. In the front hall is a photograph of one of the Burn's most illustrious visitors—Ulysses S. Grant—who had his picture taken standing on the porch during the Civil War. The Walworth family returned to their home in 1865 at the end of the war.

In 1978, the Burn was converted into a bed-and-breakfast. The guest rooms are furnished in the fashion of the time to re-create the beauty of the home at the height of its splendor. The house also contains china and a dining table that belonged to John Walworth's family. The brick walkway leads to a two-acre garden, resplendent with camellias, dogwoods and azaleas. Some guests say the owners' efforts to re-create the past have succeeded too well.

Guests who have stayed at the bed-and-breakfast claim that the old house is haunted. One of the apparitions is a group of three or four Union soldiers who appear in the back of the swimming pool. The men appear to be deep in conversation. The ghost of a little blond girl is said to disturb the sleep of guests in one of the rooms. She could be the ghost of one of the two Walworth children who died in the house during one of the city's outbreaks of yellow fever. Perhaps the process of restoring and converting the old home into a bed-and-breakfast aroused its dormant spirits, a result that seems to be the case in bed-and-breakfasts throughout the South.

The owners promote the Burn as "history in a cozy setting." Indeed, the rooms come with such twentieth-century amenities as flat-screen televisions, air conditioning and full baths. Guests are treated to wine in the evening and to a full breakfast consisting of eggs, biscuits, bacon, sausage and fruit. The ghosts are an unadvertised perk.

Natchez City Cemetery

Natchez's old burying ground was located on a hill in what is now downtown Natchez, near Memorial Park and St. Mary's Cathedral. One of the people buried here was Samuel Brooks, who served as the first mayor of Natchez from 1803 to 1811. Mayor Brooks's casket is one of the few in the old burying ground that was not moved when Natchez City Cemetery was established in 1821 on the north side of the city on a bluff overlooking the Mississippi River. The city purchased the first part of the new cemetery—approximately ten acres—from Colonel John Steel for $1,000. Plots were sold for $15 apiece. The cemetery was divided up into one section for Roman Catholics, one section for "strangers," one for "persons of color" and one for white people in general. Tombstones engraved with dates prior to 1800 mark the graves of bodies that were moved from the old burying ground and from churchyards and plantation graveyards. A number of prominent people are buried in Natchez City Cemetery, including Don Jose Vidal, governor of Natchez Spanish District in 1798; General John A. Quitman, hero of the Mexican War; and Brigadier General Charles G. Dahlgren, commander of the Third Mississippi Regiment, CSA. Natchez City Cemetery is renowned for its wrought-iron fences, its decorative benches, its iron mausoleum doors and its beautiful marble monuments, most of which were created by Edwin Lyon and Robert Rawes. Natchez City Cemetery is also famous for its fascinating legends.

The most famous monument in the Natchez City Cemetery is the Turning Angel, which was erected to commemorate one of the city's worst catastrophes. On March 14, 1908, a terrible explosion completely destroyed the Natchez Drug Company at the corner of Main and South Union Streets. The owner of the drug company bought a plot in the Natchez City Cemetery for the five girls who died in the explosion. The youngest girl was only twelve years old. He also paid for the monument of the grieving angel that was placed at the grave. The inscription on the monument reads, "Erected by the Natchez Drug Company to the memory of the unfortunate employees who lost their lives in the great disaster that destroyed its building on March 14, 1908." The sculptor carved the statue in such a way that the face of the angel appears to turn toward visitors as they approach it. The monument was made famous in a novel by Natchez native Greg Iles entitled *Turning Angel*.

Another unusual monument marks the grave of Rufus E. Case, who died at Wallenstein, Louisiana, on November 29, 1858. Case's monument resembles a wedding cake with its three tiers stacked one on top of the other.

The story goes that Case was buried sitting up in his rocking chair, not far from the grave of a child in his family, who had preceded him in death.

The strangest grave in Natchez City Cemetery is that of Florence Irene Ford, who was born on September 3, 1861. The child died of yellow fever at the age of ten on October 30, 1871. Her mother, who was understandably devastated by the death of her little girl, hated the thought of being separated from her forever. She instructed the workmen to construct a set of concrete stairs leading six feet down inside the grave. A specially installed glass pane enabled her to look at her daughter's coffin. The story goes that Florence hated thunderstorms when she was alive, so when dark clouds appeared in the sky, her mother climbed down the steps and sat by her coffin until the storm dissipated.

Technically, Natchez City Cemetery is not a haunted site. The Turning Angel is nothing more than an optical illusion. Generations of children and teenagers have frightened one another by pretending to hear weeping inside Florence Ford's grave during thunderstorms. Ironically, none of the stories that people have invented about Natchez City Cemetery are as intriguing as the truth.

PASCAGOULA

The Longfellow House

In 1850, a slave trader from New Orleans named Daniel Smith Graham built a beautiful mansion in Pascagoula, facing the Gulf of Mexico. He called his home Bellevue, but over the years, the house has come to be known as the Longfellow House because of a local legend that the poet Henry Wadsworth Longfellow visited the Grahams. However, according to Longfellow's biographers, the poet never traveled any farther south than Washington, D.C. Most likely, the rumor started because Longfellow mentioned Pascagoula in his poem "The Building of the Ship." The Longfellow House remained a private residence until the 1940s, when it was converted into a resort hotel. The historic home has also housed a girls' school and a club owned by Ingalls Shipbuilding. By the 1990s, the house was an abandoned wreck, a pathetic shadow of its former self. It was saved from demolition by an attorney, Richard Scruggs, and his wife, Diane. The couple hired Robert Cangelosi of Koch and Wilson Architects to stabilize the house and to remove any modern modifications that had been made by previous owners. They eventually gave the house to the University of

Mississippi Foundation, which used the building for wedding receptions and other social functions. During Hurricane Katrina in 2005, the Longfellow House sustained some water damage but remained structurally intact. In 2006, Dr. Randy Roth, the director of inpatient physician services at Singing River Hospital, and his wife, Dr. Tracy Roth, purchased the historic home.

The hauntings reported inside the Longfellow House have their source in an incident that supposedly occurred before the Civil War. Legend has it that the mistress of the house tortured an unruly slave in the attic. Somehow, the slave escaped and ran into the woods, where he died of his wounds. Afterward, the house slaves blamed the strange noises that echoed through the house at night on the restless spirit of the abused slave.

The paranormal activity in the home escalated when it served as a resort hotel. Bobbie Slaughter, who worked there as a night auditor during the 1980s, was alone in one of the rooms late one evening when someone slapped her face. She was struck so hard that the impression of a pink handprint was clearly visible on her face. Bobbie was ready to accuse her co-worker of hitting her until she realized that she was the only one in the room. On a different occasion, a member of the staff was trying to show a room to a couple when suddenly she fell to her knees. The young woman was convinced that someone had either tripped her or dragged her down to her knees.

Susan soon discovered that other ghosts occasionally make their presence known inside the Longfellow House. Staff members working the night shift have heard toilets flushing on their own inside empty rooms, doors opening and closing, babies crying, glasses tinkling and people laughing and talking on the upper floor. Several times, the jukebox started playing at 3:00 a.m. and did not stop until two hours later. Shadowy figures have been seen flitting along hallways and across rooms. A priest-like figure dressed in black has been seen sitting at the piano on the third floor and walking down the stairs. The strong odor of whiskey has wafted across specific parts of the hotel. Bartenders have reported glasses shattering in the bar for no apparent reason. Objects like lighted cigarettes have been placed in one room and reappeared in another location.

The paranormal activity ceased after the hotel resort closed. However, when the contractors began renovating the Longfellow House in the 1990s, the ghosts seemed to have returned. One of the workers, Andy Tillman, reported a number of strange occurrences, such as creaking noises and doors slamming shut when he was the only one in the house. Could it be that it just took a while for the ghosts to become accustomed to the new appearance of the Longfellow House?

Vicksburg

Stained Glass Manor

Fannie Vick Willis Johnson, the builder of Stained Glass Manor, was a direct descendant of Burwell Vick, the founder of Vicksburg. She was born on December 3, 1853, to John and Annie Ricks. While attending St. Francis Xavier School, Fannie and her family lived at 2430 Crawford Street. Her family home became the headquarters of General Pemberton during the Siege of Vicksburg. On May 3, 1881, Fannie married Junius Ward Pemberton during the Siege of Vicksburg. Between 1881 and 1908, Fannie and Julius split their time between the Willis-Cowan House, Duff Green Mansion and Panther Burn Plantation. In 1902, Fannie and Junius hired George Washington Maher to build their dream home, Oak Hall, at 2430 Drummond Street in Vicksburg. Maher was Frank Lloyd Wright's instructor, and many of Oak Hall's architectural elements can also be found in many of the buildings Wright designed. The house's most distinctive features are the thirty-eight original stained-glass windows that adorn it. The windows were created by Louis J. Millet, the head of the Art Institute in Chicago. Several of the designs are clearly the work of one of Millet's subcontractors, Louis Comfort Tiffany. LaMantia of New Orleans created the contemporary patterns. The mansion was completed in 1908.

Fannie and Junius shared the happiest time of their lives at Oak Hall. However, in 1919, Fannie's life changed forever. Junius was killed when a tornado struck Panther Burns. She sold the plantation the same year. Fannie devoted the rest of her life to philanthropy. In 1929, the Rotary Club recognized her charity work by awarding her the Loving Cup Award. In 1931, Fannie Vick Willis Johnson passed away. The inscription on her tombstone—"She lived for others"—commemorated her selfless devotion to the people of Vicksburg. For the next thirty-five years, Oak Hall served as a widows' home, operated by the Episcopal Diocese. In 1966, Mayor Johan Holland and his wife, Sarah, bought the old house and converted it once more into a private residence. Over the next few years, a series of renters and owners inhabited Oak Hall. Then in 1995, Bill and Shirley Smollen became the trustees of the nonprofit Stained Glass Manor–Oak Hall Historic Association. Today, Shirley Smollen operates Stained Glass Manor as a bed-and-breakfast. When the Smollens opened Stained Glass Manor to the public, they knew that the old house was rich in history, but they did not dream that some of that history was still roaming the halls.

In an interview with Sheila Turnage, Bill Smollen, a retired systems engineer for NASA, said that the bed-and-breakfast had not been open for very long before he and Shirley began receiving complaints from guests about the "noisy ghosts" that were keeping them awake all night. Bill began taking these reports seriously when items like tape measures and cameras were mysteriously moved from one location to another. The disturbances finally became so frequent that the Smollens had the house exorcised in 1996 or 1997.

Bill Smollen said that after the exorcism, the paranormal activity in Stained Glass Manor died down considerably. The only really active spirit inside the house now is the ghost of Fannie Vick. Fannie's apparition has been seen in the front yard, but her ghost usually appears in the Fannie Vick Room. Her ghost has been seen ten or eleven times in her room since the bed-and-breakfast opened. Bill said that eyewitnesses have described her ghost as having long brown hair and wearing a white robe. Guests who are especially sensitive to the paranormal have found it difficult to stay in Fannie's room. Shirley Smollen told Sheila Turnage that grown men have walked into Fannie's room, turned around and walked right back out again. Without exception, all of these men have had near-death experiences at some point in their lives. Shirley added that a number of children who were touring the house also found it difficult to stay in the Fannie Vick Room. Because Fannie Vick's ghost is such a strong presence, a number of guests have captured orbs with their digital cameras in her room.

On another occasion, two elderly ladies who had come to Vicksburg to gamble in the casinos decided to spend a night at Stained Glass Manor. Shirley Smollen said that later that evening, the two women returned to their room after a hard day's gambling. They were lying in bed when all of a sudden, the bed started shaking. Each lady accused the other of shaking the bed. The next day, the ladies told Shirley what had happened to them the night before. Shirley is convinced that Fannie Vick, who was a devout Christian, expressed her disapproval of the ladies' love of gambling by waking them up.

Although Fannie Vick's spirit has startled people in the past, her ghost has also been a comforting presence. Shirley Smollen said that one day in the late 1990s, a woman who was experiencing some severe problems booked Fannie Vick's Room for the night. Her health was bad, and she had financial problems. To make matters worse, her marriage was on the rocks.

She was unpacking her suitcase when suddenly she felt herself enveloped in warmth. The woman told Shirley that it felt like someone was giving her a big hug. She got the impression that something was trying to tell her that everything was going to be all right. Immediately, the woman's depression was alleviated. Shirley believes that Fannie Vick's ghost sensed that the woman was suffering and tried to comfort her.

Apparently, Fannie does not restrict her movements to her bedroom. Shirley Smollen said that one night in the early 2000s, a retired colonel was staying in the room right next door to Fannie Vick's bedroom. The colonel said that he was lying in bed reading when the door to the room opened, and a striking young woman walked in. She had long brown hair and was wearing a white dress. The colonel said that the woman took a few steps into the room, turned around and walked back out again. The colonel's description of the woman has convinced Shirley that he met the ghost of Fannie Vick.

Another very haunted room in Stained Glass Manor is the attic on the third floor. Bill Smollen told Sheila Turnage that in the late 1990s, a group of paranormal investigators were using a magnetometer to measure electromagnetic impulses in the room when suddenly the needle began spiking to absurd levels. The investigators interpreted the extreme fluctuations in the electromagnetic field as a sign that some very traumatic event occurred in the attic room sometime in the past. Before Shirley and Bill had bought the house, they had heard that a boy had died in the attic room of heat stroke. However, after talking to an elderly resident of Vicksburg, Shirley now believes that this residual energy was produced by a horrific murder that is rumored to have taken place in Stained Glass Manor in the 1920s. The story goes that a thirteen-year-old autistic boy was murdered in the attic room by two female occupants of the house. Shirley Smollen said that the women killed him because they feared that he would become sexually aggressive when he grew older. Some residents of Vicksburg believe that one of the women was Fannie Vick, who helped a friend of hers kill the child because they feared that he would be unable to care for himself when he became an adult. In the early 2000s, an artist who was spending the night in the attic room fell asleep and dreamed that he was a thirteen-year-old boy. The artist said that in his dream, he was awakened when two ladies entered his room. They had hairstyles from the 1920s and wore white, high-necked blouses and long, dark skirts. One of the women grabbed a pillow and shoved it in his face. Both women put their weight on the pillow and smothered the boy. The artist had not heard about the alleged murder in the attic room before he had his dream.

Other guests have had strange experiences in the attic room. One evening, a woman who had brought her young son with her to Stained Glass Manor asked the little boy if he would mind staying in the attic room by himself while she and her husband went out for the evening. The child said that he did not mind at all because there was a little boy up in the room who could play with him. On another occasion, a woman who was staying in the attic room came running down the stairs and almost knocked Shirley down. Shirley asked the woman what was wrong, and she said that she had returned to her room after lunch. As soon as she walked in the door, she began feeling very cold. Then she heard a man's voice coming from the bathroom. The woman said he seemed to be singing to himself while he was taking a bath. Shirley accompanied the woman back to the attic room, but no male intruders could be found.

Shirley feels a special bond with at least two of the spirits in her house. After her father died, she walked into her living room and was surprised to see the rocking chair rocking all by itself. Not long after the death of her husband, Bill, she was trying to type a letter to a judge on her electric typewriter and had difficulty getting the keys to work properly. Shirley's grandson, who had stopped by for a visit, sat down and started typing, and the typewriter worked perfectly. After her grandson left, Shirley told her husband's ghost to "stop playing around." She has not had any problems with the typewriter since then.

Occasionally, strange things happen that cannot be credited to a specific ghost. Lights flicker on and off, especially the light on the ceiling fan in the den on the second floor. Several times, something has set off the motion detector, but no human trespassers have ever been found. Sometimes when Shirley is in the house all by herself, she hears someone walking on the second floor. In the late 2000s, Shirley had just walked in the front door when she saw a woman wearing a large peony walk out of the dining room and up the staircase. Shirley followed the woman up the stairs but was unable to find her anywhere in the house. When I was staying at Stained Glass Manor in July 2009, Shirley pointed to an African American doll that was nestled in a pile of dolls sitting on the floor next to the side door. "Two years ago, that doll disappeared," Shirley said. "I looked for it everywhere and couldn't find it. Two years later, I was headed out the door, and I just happened to look at the dolls on the floor. There it was, back in its usual place. I don't know what happened to it." A Bible belonging to a lady from Alabama who used to cook for the Smollens also holds deep significance for Shirley. "I don't

The ghost of Fannie Vick is said to still walk the halls of Stained Glass Manor. *Courtesy of the author.*

know why I have that lady's Bible," Shirley said. "But a prayer that was placed inside the Bible just knocked me out. It was a prayer that I needed at a particular moment."

One would think that residing in a haunted house would be unnerving for a woman who is living all by herself. However, Shirley has never really felt threatened by any of the spirits in the house, especially the ghost of Fannie Vick. She agrees with her late husband, Bill, who described Fannie Vick as being "very, very loving."

North Carolina

Asheville

Chicken Alley

Chicken Alley, a small, narrow alley in Downtown Asheville, is one of the most picturesque sites in the city. The old brick walls of the surrounding buildings are colorfully decorated with street art, including the highly stylized likenesses of giant chickens, birds, frogs, Yoda and Frankenstein's monster. Chicken Alley's greatest claim to fame, however, is the ghost that haunts the location.

Dr. Jamie Smith was a prominent physician in Asheville at the turn of the century. His trademark look consisted of a black fedora, a long coat, a medicine bag and a cane. Even though he gave the appearance of being an upstanding citizen, he was also known to frequent Asheville's rowdier nightspots. Ironically, the treatment of social diseases made up much of Dr. Smith's practice.

Dr. Smith's love of the nightlife eventually led to his downfall. One evening in 1902, Dr. Smith entered Broadway's Tavern in Chicken Alley at the same time two of the patrons were engaged in a serious argument. Dr. Smith tried to break up the fight but was stabbed in the heart by one of the combatants.

Dr. Smith's ghost has been seen strolling down Chicken Alley for over a century. The description given by eyewitnesses always includes a black hat, duster coat, black medicine bag and a cane with a silver head. Apparently, the good doctor's love of a good time was so strong that it even transcended death.

The Biltmore Estate

The Biltmore Estate is the largest privately owned residence in the United States. It was built by George Washington Vanderbilt in 1888. After Vanderbilt died in 1914, his widow, Edith, and his daughter, Cornelia, inherited the property. A few years later, financial difficulties forced Edith to sell 125,000 acres to the federal government. Later, Pisgah National Forest was created from the Vanderbilt land. By 1930, Edith's fortunes had declined so drastically that she had to open her magnificent home to the general public. Celebrities who have toured the Biltmore Estate include Tom Hanks, Teddy Roosevelt and Jackie Kennedy.

Today, many of the spirited sightings at the Biltmore Estate have taken place during the house tours. People have heard the boisterous sounds of a pool party, even though the pool was empty at the time. Some

Biltmore Estate in Asheville, North Carolina. *Courtesy of the Library of Congress.*

guests have reported hearing whispered conversations. The full-bodied apparition of George Vanderbilt has been seen reading in the library. Several employees have been tripped by an invisible foot while walking through the Banquet Hall.

Some of the most startling encounters inside the old mansion were experienced by an employee named L.A. Stewart. He had just started working at the Biltmore Estate when he had a very bizarre sighting. He had crossed the courtyard and was about to enter the stable shops when he saw the lower half of a reddish-brown horse standing in the hallway. He said that he also heard the clopping sounds of horses' hooves inside the stable shops.

One of the most haunted parts of the house is the area between the Brown Laundry and the floral department. Stewart was walking through the basement hallway one afternoon when he saw the figure of a middle-aged woman walk into the floral room. She had a very stern, businesslike expression on her face. He suspects that the mysterious woman was Mrs. King, George Vanderbilt's head housekeeper.

The abundance of spirits in a house the size of the Biltmore is understandable considering the large number of people who worked there every day. The frequent appearance of some of the servants testifies to their undying devotion to the Vanderbilt family.

BOONE

Appalachian State University

In 1895, a group of citizens under the leadership of two brothers, Blanford B. and Dauphine D. Dougherty, initiated a campaign to educate teachers in northwestern North Carolina. On October 5, 1903, the Appalachian Training School for Teachers opened its doors with 325 students. In 1929, the newly named Appalachian State Teachers College became a four-year degree-granting institution. In 1967, the institution acquired university status when it expanded to include other programs. In 1971, Appalachian State University became part of the University of North Carolina system. It is now the sixth-largest university within the system. Although much has changed over the years, one constant at the school is the ghost stories students tell about Coffee Residence Hall and East Hall Dormitory.

Two ghosts are said to be haunting Coffee Residence Hall. One of them is a ghost named Max. He is the spirit of a professor who committed suicide in Room 311 when the building was a residence hall for faculty. The other ghost is known as the "White Lady." She has been seen by residents and housekeepers floating outside the windows on the second and third floors.

The ghost of East Hall is the spirit of a student who committed suicide in the basement area known as the "Dungeon." In the earliest version of the tale, a female student hanged herself in the basement restroom with a silk scarf. Today, students tell the story of the ghost of a suicidal young man. It is unclear whether these are two versions of the same legend or two entirely different stories.

A number of manifestations have taken place in East Hall, making it the most haunted dormitory at Appalachian State University. Students have reported hearing maniacal laughter in the basement. The burned impression of a noose has appeared several times on the bathroom ceiling in the Dungeon. Recent reports of paranormal activity include the sighting of a tall, scruffy-looking young man on the subfloor. Some years ago, several young men saw the apparition walk into one of the rooms. Because the boys knew this was not the student who lived in that room, they contacted the resident assistant. When he opened the door, the room was empty, and the windows were locked from the inside. The ghost showed up once again during the cleanup of a Halloween party. He walked through the door of the room and into the hallway, where he vanished. One of the students recognized him as the mysterious young man who had appeared in the subfloor room two weeks before.

Chatham County

The Devil's Tramping Grounds

One of North Carolina's most infamous legends is set in a remote spot in the woods near Harper's Crossroads, just ten miles south of Siler City. A worn path off Devil's Tramping Ground Road leads to a barren circle that is forty feet in diameter. Nothing but a few weeds and sprigs of grass can be detected within the circle. The strange clearing was first discovered by early settlers in Chatham County just before the Revolutionary War. For generations, people living in the area passed down the story that the devil walks around in circles at night as he ponders new ways to entrap humanity. Any plants hardy enough to germinate within the circle eventually wither and die. Locals also say that any object that was placed in the circle before sundown will be found outside of the circle at dawn. The few men brave enough to spend the night in the Devil's Tramping Ground were driven insane. Even dogs refuse to walk into the circle.

A number of explanations have been given for the strange, barren circle over the years. The early setters believed that the Indians created the circle for use in their rituals. Others say that horses or mules walked around in a circle grinding grain many years ago. These theories have been dismissed because similar spots have been overgrown with plant life. The best explanation was provided by scientists who discovered that the ground is sterile.

MONROE

Blakeney House

The stately house standing at 418 East Franklin Street was built by Charles C. Cook. One of the first owners, William Blakeney, was a banker who was rumored to have hid his money somewhere in the house. Blakeney came to an untimely end when he died in an automobile accident. The Blakeney family continued living in the house throughout most of the twentieth century. In 1989, Pat Lilly became the first outsider to own the house. She converted the house into a restaurant called Boswell's, which closed in August 1994. Today, the house is occupied by Youth with a Mission (YWAM), which provides Bible and missionary training for teenagers.

Many of the ghost stories originated in the years when Pat Lilly ran a restaurant there. Pat Lilly said that she saw the apparition of a little girl on several occasions. A businessman who was unfamiliar with the restaurant's haunted reputation began talking to the little girl. He was surprised when she simply faded away because he thought she was real. The ghosts of William Blakeney and of a woman in a red dress have also manifested inside the Blakeney House.

A great deal of poltergeist-like activity has been reported inside the Blakeley House as well. Guests have reported seeing candles ignite themselves. Cool breezes have been known to waft through the house when all of the windows are closed. Doors that were locked before closing were found unlocked the next morning. Disembodied footsteps have been heard inside.

It is important to note that not everyone who has spent time inside the Blakeley House believes it is haunted. In 2011, YWAM director Todd Hedgepeth said that he had worked inside the old house for seven years and never encountered anything out of the ordinary. "We are not interested in perpetuating the story," Hedgepeth said.

RUTHERFORD

Chimney Rock

Hickory Nut Gorge is North Carolina's most striking gateway to the western mountains. Standing above the gorge is a three-hundred-foot-tall monolith called Chimney Rock. In 1902, Dr. Lucius B. Morse and his two brothers purchased Chimney Rock and the eight hundred surrounding acres. The village of Chimney Rock, which has spread out through the gorge, is sustained by the flocks of tourists who travel to Rutherford to catch a glimpse of one of North Carolina's best-known landmarks. Since the toll road first opened in 1916, over one million people have visited Chimney Rock to catch the spectacular view of Lake Lure and the surrounding countryside.

On July 31, 1806, a much smaller crowd was treated to an even more unbelievable sight at Chimney Rock. An eight-year-old girl named Elizabeth Reaves and her older brother, Morgan, were treated to the spectacle of thousands of people in white gowns flying around Chimney Rock. The children called to their mother, Patsy Reeves, and their sister, Polly, who were joined by four other neighbors. In an article published a few weeks later in the *Raleigh Register and Gazette*, the witnesses reported seeing thousands of white-clad beings fly to the top of Chimney Rock. After a few minutes, three of the figures led the others into the sky, where they disappeared. The entire incredible episode lasted one hour.

In 1811, a similar spectacle took place above Chimney Rock. A large number of people claimed to have seen a heavenly battle between two armies of cavalry, the men slashing at one another with sabers. During the ten-minute battle, witnesses heard the moans of wounded and dying and the unmistakable clang of metal against metal. Before dissipating into the darkness, the ghostly armies had wrought such an indelible impression on the spectators that newspapers across the United States ran the story. Locals wonder when—or if—the apparitions at Chimney Rock will return.

SOUTH CAROLINA

ABBEVILLE

Abbeville Opera House

At the turn of the century, road companies traveled throughout the country, regaling audiences with shows that had completed their New York engagements. For years, Abbeville was an overnight stopping point for tours traveling from New York to Richmond and Atlanta. In the early 1900s, a group of citizens campaigned for the building of an opera house in Abbeville. Work on the 7,500-square-foot Abbeville Opera House was completed in 1908. Between 1908 and 1913, the citizens of Abbeville were treated to 260 minstrel, vaudeville and burlesque shows. Even the Ziegfeld Follies performed here. Between 1914 and 1930, the live performances were replaced with silent movies. Movies continued to be shown at the Abbeville Opera House until the 1950s, when it closed its doors, a victim of the television age.

In 1958, the Abbeville Community Theater group was formed to revive live theater in the town. The restoration of the abandoned Abbeville Opera House began in 1968. Once again, Abbeville became the theatrical hub of the Upstate region of South Carolina. Today, the opera house looks much the same as it did when it first opened in 1908. Even the same rope is used to pull rigging systems. The only concessions to the modern age are rocking chair seats and air conditioning.

The Abbeville Opera House became known as a haunted theater after it reopened in the late 1960s. During the restoration of the old building, all the chairs in the balcony were removed except one, the "ghost chair." When the lights went out or the curtain got stuck, the blame was placed on the solitary chair. Workers would not even touch the chair for fear that something would go wrong with the productions.

Full-bodied apparitions have been sighted in the balcony. In her book *Haunted Theaters of the Carolinas*, author Cheralyn Lambeth said that during a curtain call of a play, an actor saw a lone woman dressed in old-fashioned clothing standing in the balcony, clapping. After that sighting, phantom applause has been heard several times in the balcony. Employees of the theater believe that this could be the spirit of an actress who died shortly after performing at the theater in the 1920s. Members of the African American community in Abbeville tell a much different story. They say that in the 1930s, a black man who was dating a white woman was murdered in the balcony. Whoever the ghost is, he or she does not seem to be willing to quiet down anytime soon.

Camden

Old Quaker Cemetery

Quakers began settling in what is now Camden in 1750. In 1759, Samuel Wyly designated four acres of land for use as a cemetery. The Quakers rented the land for "One Pepper Corn Per Year" for 999 years. The cemetery has grown to fifty acres, mostly as the result of donations and purchases of land. The town deeded the cemetery to the Quaker Cemetery Association in 1874. People from all works of life—Quakers, merchants, veterans of wars and ministers—are interred here. Some of the most famous people buried here include Abraham Lincoln's brother-in-law, several Confederate generals and a Civil War hero known as the "Angel of Marye's Heights." However, no one in the cemetery is more legendary than Agnes of Glasgow.

Agnes of Glasgow was born in Scotland in 1760. When she was twenty years old, she fell in love with Angus McPherson, a lieutenant in the British army. After he was shipped across the Atlantic to fight the Patriots in the Revolutionary War, she stowed away on a ship bound for the colonies. When she arrived in Charleston, she learned that Lieutenant McPherson had been transferred to Camden. Unfortunately, by the time she arrived in Camden, her lover was nowhere to be found. She scoured the woods and towns in the area in search of Lieutenant McPherson. Before she was able to locate him, she was struck down with an illness and died. She was buried in Quaker Cemetery in 1780.

Agnes of Glasgow may be dead, but her legend lives on. People throughout South Carolina are familiar with her tragic story. Her grave has become a favorite of ghost hunters eager to make contact with the legendary figure. Their quest is spurred by the local belief that she walks through the graveyard in search of her lost love.

Hilton Head

Baynard Plantation Ruins

The mansion house at Baynard Plantation on Baraddock's Point (now known as Sea Pines) was owned by two families. The first owner was John Stoney, a sea captain who arrived in South Carolina in 1774. Two years later, he bought the one-thousand-acre Braddock Point Plantation. In 1793, Stoney and his slaves built a forty- by forty-six-foot plantation house. The foundation was made of tabby, a mixture of lime, sand, water and oyster shells. After Stoney was killed in a hunting accident in 1821, his two sons, James and John, inherited the property. James died first, in 1827. By the time John, also known as "Saucy Jack," died in 1838, the plantation had been mortgaged to the Bank of Charleston.

For years, people on Hilton Head believed that William Eddings Baynard won the plantation from Saucy Jack in a poker game. Actually, he purchased the plantation from the Bank of Charleston for $10,000 in 1840. The plantation prospered under Baynard's ownership. He died in 1849 of yellow fever and was buried in a mausoleum in Zion Cemetery. His wife, who had died of dehydration and fever years before, is buried with him.

William's son, Ephram, ran the plantation until November 1861, when the Union army occupied Hilton Head Island. Ephram, along with most of his neighbors, left the island for the duration of the war. In 1864, the mansion was used as the headquarters for the Union army. Before the war

Baynard Plantation on Hilton Head Island, South Carolina. *Courtesy of the Library of Congress.*

ended, the mansion was burned, some believe, by the Confederate army. Today, nothing remains of the once-grand mansion house but the tabby foundation and a corner wall.

Locals believe that William Baynard's ghost is a restless spirit because his corpse was removed by Yankee soldiers looking for family valuables. Generations of residents of Hilton Head Island have seen a phantom funeral procession make its way down the old road past the Baynard Plantation ruins to his mausoleum. The hearse is followed by a procession of livery-clad servants. After the hearse comes to a stop, Baynard's ghost climbs down from the hearse and walks over to the gate of the mausoleum. After a few minutes of quiet meditation, he returns to the hearse and rides away. Many people believe that he is still making his daily visits to his wife's grave, just as he had done for fifteen years after her death.

St. Helena Island

The Chapel of Ease

St. Helena Island has been controlled by Spain, France, Britain and the United States because it is ideally suited to the planting of rice, indigo and spices. In the eighteenth and nineteenth centuries, huge plantations, worked mostly by slaves, sprung up all over the island. The planters and their families attended worship services at the Chapel of Ease, which was built of tabby in 1740. The planters abandoned the church in 1861, when they deserted the island. Union soldiers attended services there during the war. It was gutted by a forest fire in 1868. Today, only the shell—and the ghost stories—remain.

Some paranormal activity has been reported around the chapel itself. Visitors to the site have heard spectral voices and the melodious strains of hymns being sung from inside the chapel. A few people claim to have heard group prayers coming from the chapel as well.

The remains of the Chapel of Ease on St. Helena Island. *Courtesy of the Library of Congress.*

The cemetery behind the chapel is said to be even more haunted. During the war, Union soldiers ruined the door to the vault of Edgar and Eliza Fripp. After the war, workmen bricked up the entrance to the mausoleum. The next day, they were surprised to find that all of the bricks had been stacked up next to the vault. The police determined that no one had been in the cemetery the night before. Today, the partially bricked doorway to the mausoleum is still open. One wonders if the ghostly woman seen in the cemetery wearing a white shroud and holding a baby is the spirit of Eiliza Fripp, who still resents having her eternal rest disturbed.

The Leamington Lighthouse

Located on the Arthurs Hills Golf Course, the Leamington Lighthouse was built between 1879 and 1880. It was originally part of a series of navigation lights that had been constructed to guide ships safely into Port Royal Sound. In the nineteenth century, the complex included the forward beacon, a rear lighthouse and a keeper's house. The lighthouse was deactivated in 1932. However, it was mustered into service briefly during World War II as a lookout tower for enemy ships. The lighthouse was restored by Greenwood Communities and Resorts in 1985, and it is now open to the public. Today, only the ninety-four-foot rear lighthouse and a brick oil house remain. The dedication of the lighthouse keepers is memorialized in the legend of the Blue Lady.

In 1898, Hilton Head was buffeted by a devastating hurricane. The lighthouse keeper, Adam Fripp, struggled to keep the light burning in the high winds. Suddenly, he grabbed his chest and collapsed, the victim of a heart attack. His twenty-one-year-old daughter, Corline, helped him to the keeper's house and put him in bed. As he lay dying, he clasped Caroline's hands and asked her to keep the light burning. She promised she would and kept the light burning throughout the remainder of the storm. When high winds came up, she put on her blue dress and walked around the island warning people of high tides. Some people say that she died three weeks after her father's death. Others say that she lived a long life. For years thereafter, people have seen the form of a woman in a blue dress walking the grounds surrounding the lighthouse. Apparently, Corline is still at her post, just as her father had asked.

Tennessee

Bolivar

Magnolia Manor

Magnolia Manor was built in 1849 by Judge Austin Miller. He has been credited with establishing the southern boundary of the state in such a way that Memphis is now located in Tennessee instead of Mississippi. The bricks used to build the two-story Georgia Colonial mansion were made by slaves on the plantation. The house has thirteen-inch-thick walls, fourteen-foot ceilings, four bedrooms and double parlors. In 1862, Magnolia Manor became the headquarters for the Union army. Generals Logan, McPherson, Sherman and Grant are said to have planned the Battle of Shiloh within the walls of this mansion. Mrs. Miller allowed them to use only half of the mansion. The story goes that during dinner, General Sherman said that all Southern men, women and children should be exterminated. Mrs. Miller was so upset that she rushed out to the back porch. General Grant followed her and asked her why she was crying. When she told him what General Sherman had said, he returned to the parlor and ordered Sherman to apologize to the lady. Sherman did as he was told but was so irate that as he was walking up the staircase to his room, he removed his sabre and slashed the bannister. The cut mark is still visible.

Built in 1849 by Judge Austin Miller, Magnolia Manor is said to be the place where General Ulysses S. Grant planned the Battle of Shiloh. *Courtesy of the author.*

The Millers' children also became prominent figures in the history of Tennessee. Their son, Charles Austin Miller, became the secretary of state of Tennessee. A daughter, Lizzie Lea Miller, was the first woman in Tennessee to be elected state representative.

In 1985, Magnolia Manor was converted into a bed-and-breakfast by Elaine Cox. Although governors and even a vice president have spent the night at the bed-and-breakfast, Magnolia Manor's most fascinating occupants are its ghosts.

Since Elaine Cox first took over Magnolia Manor in the 1980s, a number of paranormal events have occurred here, including disembodied footsteps, antique dolls moving on their own and doors opening and closing. Personal experiences have been reported in each of the guest rooms. In the C.A. Miller Suite, a guest was awakened at 3:00 a.m. by the creaking of a rocking chair. For just a few seconds, the ghost of a woman appeared in the rocking chair before dissipating completely. In 2008, Elaine Cox was standing in the Judge Austin Miller Suite during one of the mansion's ghost tours when she saw a shimmering shape the size of a human being move up and down on the bed. The ghost of an African

American woman has been sighted inside the Cottage, which was used as slave quarters and a kitchen before the Civil War. In the 1849 Room, a man was awakened by a female apparition pulling on his shirt sleeve. The man ran out of the room and left the bed-and-breakfast without his luggage. A woman was asleep in Annie's Room when someone began pulling the covers off the bed. When she woke up, she saw an elderly woman holding a candle standing at the foot of the bed.

I spent the night at Magnolia Manor on June 13–14, 2014. After my wife, Marilyn, and I took our suitcases up to the 1849 Room, we sat on the front porch and sipped wine while Tom Gatti, Elaine's husband, regaled us with ghost stories about the mansion:

> *When we purchased this house in the 1980s, we didn't know it was haunted. We suspected that something strange was going on inside the house—pots and pans moved, and the key in the door turned by itself—but we didn't know for sure until a psychic from Natchez named Jan Limley called me up and asked to investigate the house with several of her friends. I said, "Sure. Come on."*
>
> *After they arrived, she came up to me and said, "I'll put my hands on different objects and talk to the spirits. Why don't y'all do your own thing and just let me do mine."*
>
> *She walked into the 1849 Room, the most haunted room in the mansion, and asked if she could touch the portrait hanging over the fireplace. The portrait is a picture of Priscilla, who died when she was eighteen years old. I told her she could and left the room. She was in the room with six other people when suddenly the portrait flew off the wall like a shot! Elaine is a skeptic, and she thought Jan was playing a trick, so she examined Jan's hands, but she couldn't find anything unusual. I always get an eerie feeling when I walk into this room.*

This portrait of an eighteen-year-old girl named Priscilla flew from its place above the fireplace mantle during a paranormal investigation. *Courtesy of the author.*

Tom went on to say that Priscilla's ghost has pulled the covers off guests while they are sleeping. She also plays with the coat hangers in the wardrobe. One of Tom's sons had a firsthand experience with Priscilla's playful side. Tom said, "There is a doll of an old man sitting in a little chair by the door. Usually, his arms are crossed. One night when my son was staying in the room, he woke up to find that the doll's arms were hanging by his sides. It really spooked him."

The cottage is a small brick building that served as a cookhouse and as the slave quarters before the Civil War. Tom said that the full-bodied apparition of the cook, Adeline, has been seen several times. Over the past couple of years, a ghostly parrot has been seen and heard inside the cottage as well. The specter of a ghost cat is another frequent guest inside the old building.

"One of the Millers' daughters, Annie, had a cat," Tom said. "She was a wild child. When her cat died, she took it down to Polk cemetery, which is very private, and buried him. They told her she couldn't bury the cat there, so she dug him up and took him to the pet cemetery. A few months later, they

Originally used as the cookhouse, this brick cottage is haunted by the ghosts of a cat, a parrot and an African American cook named Adeline. *Courtesy of the author.*

Guests staying in the 1849 Room have had their feet tickled and the covers pulled off the bed by a pair of invisible hands. Orbs can be seen to the left and above the wardrobe. *Courtesy of the author.*

relented and told her that she could bury the cat in Polk Cemetery. The cat is in the Miller Family Plot, and he even has his own tombstone."

Ghostly activity has also occurred in the dining room. "We have a ghost we call 'Old Smokey' in the dining room," Tom said. "Old Smokey sometimes walks from the dining room and walks down the hall to our room. He hardly ever comes in, but once in a while, Elaine sees this silhouette in the bedroom."

The den, which is connected to the dining room, is also haunted, possibly by Old Smokey. "One night, the den appeared to be full of people, and most of them were in Civil War uniforms, smoking cigars. One guy seemed to be making the rounds of the room. [These ghosts] were visible for almost a minute. I couldn't believe it! People still say they smell cigar smoke back there."

After Tom finished his stories, Marilyn and I went to bed in the 1849 Room. At 2:00 a.m., she got up to go to the bathroom. After she returned to bed, she was lying on her side when she felt something touching her arm. "It was like somebody was lightly brushing it with their hand," Marilyn said.

The next night, she and I took photographs throughout the room in the hope of catching something. I did not get anything, but Marilyn photographed several orbs floating around the wardrobe.

One third of the guests at Magnolia Manor are paranormal investigators. A paranormal group called the Memphis Ghost Hunters has investigated Magnolia Manor several times since 2004. Because the mansion is so haunted, the group has been offering training workshops to interested ghost hunters at Magnolia Manor since 2006. In October, ghost tours of Bolivar leave from Magnolia Manor. Ghosts can be troublesome, and even terrifying, but they can also be profitable.

Chapel Hill

Chapel Hill Light

Like many ghost lights in the South, the Chapel Hill Light is part of the local railroad lore. Legend has it that one night in the late nineteenth century, a brakeman was walking along the tops of the railroad cars, applying the brakes to each one, when the train lurched suddenly. He was thrown onto the rails, where he was decapitated. In another version of the tale, a man who was accustomed to riding the train at night was standing on the railroad tracks, signaling the engineer with a lantern, just as he always did. On this particular night, however, the train had a new engineer who did not see the man's swinging lantern in time and ran over him. In yet another version, a train had derailed, and a signalman was standing on the tracks, signaling an oncoming train with his lantern to slow down. The train hit the signalman, killing him instantly. Some people say the signalman tripped and fell on the tracks, knocking himself unconscious just before the train passed over him. All of the stories end with the poor man walking the rails endlessly with his lantern, looking for his lost head.

The Chapel Hill Light has been seen along the railroad tracks by many of the residents of Chapel Hill. The light has been described as a small, glowing disk that hovers four feet off the ground before blinking out. Another witness claimed to have seen three glowing lights that appeared on one side of the tracks, crossed the tracks and then vanished. There is probably a logical explanation for the Chapel Hill Light, but none of the witnesses has come up with one so far.

HICKORY VALLEY

The Ames Plantation

Of all the early settlers in Fayette County, David Jernigan was one of the most prominent. He arrived in 1823 and immediately set about creating a plantation on a large tract of land. He died in 1842 and was buried in the family plot, along with fourteen of his friends and relatives. Today, the Ames Plantation is an amalgamation of a number of old plantations that form the agricultural hub of the University of Tennessee. The residence that bears the name of the Ames Manor House was built by John W. Jones on his homestead.

Each of the plantations that make up the Ames Plantation has its own cemetery and its own ghosts. The restless spirits of people who committed suicide have been sighted on the plantation. However, the most commonly sighted ghosts on the plantation are the full-bodied apparitions of a woman and a little girl. They are believed to be the ghosts of David Jernigan's wife and daughter. Ghostly noises are also said to emanate from the cemetery. Visitors have reported hearing the sounds of workers operating the cotton gins and the gristmills. Some people have even reported hearing the unmistakable works songs and spirituals of slaves as they toil in the fields.

KINGSPORT

Rotherwood Mansion

The current Rotherwood Mansion was built in 1818 at the bend of the Holston River by a wealthy planter named Revered Frederick Ross. It was built on the site of the original Rothewood Mansion, which burned. Ross was also the founder of Rossville, which later became Kingsport. James Dobyns, the first president of the Home and Loan Company, purchased the house in 1905. It was sold once again in 1917 to John Dennis. The U.S. Army bought Rotherwood Mansion in 1941 to be used as housing for officers stationed at the Rotherwood Army Ammunitions Plant during World War II. After the war, Dennis bought the house from the army and sold it to Herbert Stone. After years of neglect, Rotherwood Mansion was sold at auction to businessman Sam Pickering, who died only a year after buying the house. Three years later, fashion designer Robert Baugh paid $270,000 for the house and began restoring the exterior of the old mansion. After Baugh died in 1989, local physician Lina Thibault bought the house for $570,000 with the intention of restoring the interior. Today, Rotherwood Mansion is a private residence that is remembered primarily for its ghost stories.

The mansion's signature ghost story focuses on Frederick Ross's daughter, Rowena. She was reputed to be a great beauty who was doted on by her father. Two years after returning from finishing school, she fell in love with a young man from a nearby town. The couple soon became engaged, and they were prepared to spend the rest of their lives together. However, fate intervened on the afternoon of their wedding day. Rowena's fiancé was in a boat, fishing with friends, when the small craft overturned. Everyone survived the accident but Rowena's lover, who drowned.

Rowena immediately secluded herself inside her father's mansion. Ten years later, Rowena married a wealthy man from Knoxville. The birth of Rowena's daughter brightened her life for a brief time, but Rowena sank into depression once again after the child died of an illness at age ten. Not long afterward, Rowena killed herself. Some people say that she plunged into the Hoston River, not far from where her fiancé had drowned. Soon, local storytellers transformed Rowena into the "Lady in White," a mournful spirit who walks along the riverbank, searching for her lost love.

Legend has it that Rowena's father became bankrupt not long after his daughter's death and was forced to sell Rotherwood Mansion to a cruel slave owner named Joshua Phipps in 1847. People living nearby said that they could hear the screams of his slaves as they suffered under the lash. The sadistic Phipps was even rumored to have installed a whipping post inside his house. Because of his unsavory reputation, Phipps's neighbors avoided him. One day, Phipps contracted a mysterious illness and was confined to a bed in the carriage house. A slave who tended to Phipps said that he was lying in bed when all at once a swarm of black flies flew into room. The flies covered Phipps's eyes and mouth, smothering him.

Even though Phipps was hated by the community, a large number of people attended his funeral, more out of curiosity than out of respect for the dead. The stories go that after the casket was loaded into the hearse, the wheels refused to move. Then, as dark clouds blotted out the sun, a black dog emerged from underneath the canopy covering the casket and leaped off the hearse.

Not surprisingly, Joshua Phipps's spirit is not at rest. His insane laughter and piercing screams have resounded through the halls of Rotherwood Mansion for many years. He has been identified as the entity that pulls the covers off sleeping occupants of the house. He is an annoying presence that hides objects and stares through the windows. The scratching sounds and disembodied footsteps that have disturbed the tranquility of the mansion for years have also been attributed to the cruel slaveholder.

NASHVILLE

The Capitol Records Building

The Capitol Records Building at 3322 West End Avenue was built on the site of the Schnell House. Joseph Schnell was a wealthy businessman who built his lavish mansion in 1900 in what is now Music Row. Despite his family's opulent lifestyle, Schnell's two daughters were never accepted by any of the other upper-class young women in Nashville. Because of their status as social outcasts, the girls never married. They inherited the Schnell House and all of their father's wealth after his death. The sisters rarely ventured outside their house, which fell into disrepair, and they eventually died inside of it. In the absence of heirs, the State of Tennessee took over the house and property. The property was then sold to Capitol Records, which razed the old Schnell House and built a gray, eleven-story office building on the site. Capitol Records occupies only the eleventh floor; the other floors in the building have been rented out to other businesses.

The Schnell House may be gone, but the spirits of the Schnell family still remain on the property, especially on the eleventh floor. Computers and other types of electronic equipment malfunction for no apparent reason. Doors open and close on their own. Spectral laughter, phantom footsteps and faint whispers have been heard throughout the eleventh floor. Items that have been placed in one location are found in an entirely different spot the next day.

Sightings of the full-bodied apparitions of Joseph Schnell and his daughters have also been reported on the eleventh floor of the Capitol Records Building. Some people believe their manifestations and the poltergeist-like activity reflect the family's displeasure at having their beautiful home replaced by a bland office building.

PURDY

The Hurst House

In 1834, Fielding Hurst moved to McNairy County. By 1850, the Hurst family had become one of the largest landowners in McNairy Count. The Hurst family was so influential that its members were referred to as the "Hurst nation" by their neighbors. Fielding was the self-appointed leader. He was a vocal Union sympathizer whose opposition to the secession referendum resulted in his incarceration at the state penitentiary. Fielding was freed when the Union army occupied Nashville, and he immediately set about taking revenge on the Confederacy. He formed a unit of mounted scouts whose primary mission was to patrol West Tennessee for robbers and guerrillas. After appealing to Andrew Johnson, the military governor of Tennessee, Hurst was appointed commandeer of the First West Tennessee Cavalry. His brutal tactics alarmed both secessionists and Unionists in Kentucky. Hurst's raid on Purdy, which resulted in the burning of the church, courthouse and a number of private residences, was so brutal that he was briefly arrested. Hurst and his men were also ordered to pay $5,000 for the destruction of property in Jackson, Tennessee. Confederate forces in West Tennessee retaliated by torturing Hurst's nephew and injuring his elderly sister.

Even though Hurst was constantly threatened with court-martial due to his unorthodox methods, he continued to serve as commander of the Sixth Tennessee Cavalry because his counterinsurgency operations were so effective. However, when Hurst and his regiment burned Jackson during a second raid on the city, they were transferred to middle Tennessee. Hurst resigned on December 10, 1864, because of ill health.

After the Civil War, Fielding Hurst was blamed for more atrocities than he and his men actually committed. He died bankrupt and alone in 1882. Locals vented their anger against Hurst by trampling and spitting on his grave in Mount Gilead Cemetery.

Hurst's memory lives on in the ghost stories told about his home on Gann Road in Purdy. Some historians believe the Hurst House is the oldest house in McNairy County. After Hurst's death, the house was owned by Bessie and Mary Dodds. It was purchased by Tim Cathers of Memphis, who plans to restore the heavily vandalized old house. Many teenagers are attracted to the house because of the legend that Hurst was shot at the top of the stairs. People say that bloodstains resurfaces once a year on the anniversary of Hurst's death. The story of Hurst's death is apocryphal, but the haunting might not be. At least one person has experienced camera problems when trying to take pictures in the room where Hurst is said to have died.

VIRGINIA

ABINGDON

The Martha Washington Inn

General Francis Preston spent $15,000 building his family home in 1832. The founders of Martha Washington College bought the property in 1858 and converted it into a school for women. During the Civil War, a Confederate unit called the Washington Mounted Rifles trained at the school. A number of the girls served as nurses when the school was used as a field hospital for Confederate soldiers. The dual effects of the Great Depression and a typhoid fever epidemic caused the school to close its doors in 1932. Three years later, the Martha Washington Inn opened inside the former school. A group of businessmen called the United Group bought the inn in 1984 and renovated the old mansion extensively. Today, the lobby of the inn contains a number of items once owned by the Preston family, including a Dutch-baroque grandfather clock. The family's ghosts are preserved in the legends that abound inside the Martha Washington Inn.

Two of the inn's ghost stories date back to the Civil War. One of these stories deals with a young Confederate soldier who fell in love with one of the young women enrolled in Martha Washington College. On the day he was supposed to deliver news to General Robert E. Lee regarding the activities of the Union army, he stopped at the college to say farewell to his beloved. Entering the college through a cave system under the school and a hidden stairway, the young man rushed into the waiting arms of his girlfriend. Suddenly, two Union soldiers intruded on the couple. Before he could react, the soldiers shot the young man. His sweetheart gasped as her lover lay dying in a pool of his own blood. Over the years, the bloodstain has reappeared, defying attempts to cover it up with stain. When carpeting was placed over the bloodstain, holes appeared over the stains.

The hotel's second ghost story is also set during the Civil War. A wounded Union officer named Captain John Stoves was captured and brought to the college for treatment. He was carried up to Room 217, where he was treated by a young student named Beth. She soon fell in love with the young man. He tried to persuade the girl to play a song for him, but he passed away before she could begin. Three weeks later, she died of typhoid. Many guests and employees have reported hearing the lilting strain of a violin at night.

Chatham Manor

William Fitzhugh built Chatham Manor in 1771. He named the Georgian-style home after the Earl of Chatham. The 1,280-acre plantation overlooking the Rappahannock River originally included dozens of outbuildings: a dairy, icehouse, stables, a fish hatchery and barns. Fitzhugh entertained his planter friends at the racetrack he had built on the estate. George Washington, who had served with Fitzhugh in the House of Burgesses, visited the plantation twice in the 1780s. Thomas Jefferson visited Chatham Manor on October 27, 1793. Fitzhugh was such a genial host that the crush of guests attending his parties eventually became unbearable. In 1796, he moved to Alexandria and put his mansion up for sale.

The plantation was purchased by Major Churchill Jones for $20,000. Members of the Jones family continued living in Chatham Manor for sixty-six years. A small slave insurrection took place at the plantation in 1805. An armed posse punished the five slaves responsible for the whipping of the overseer and four other people.

During the Civil War, Chatham Manor was owned by James Horace Lacy and his wife, who was the niece of Churchill Jones. Almost as soon as war was declared, Lacy enlisted in the Confederate army, leaving his wife and children in the mansion. In 1862, his family was forced to leave when Union troops occupied the house. They remained there for the next thirteen months. Seven months before the Battle of Fredericksburg, President

Abraham visited the mansion to confer with General Irwin McDowell and his staff. Following the Union army's crushing defeat at Fredericksburg, the mansion was converted into a field hospital for many of the army's twelve thousand casualties. The wounded and dying Union soldiers were treated by Clara Barton and poet Walt Whitman, who had traveled to Fredericksburg in search of his brother, who had been wounded in the battle.

By the end of the war in 1865, Chatham Manor was a wreck. The walls and floors were spotted with bloodstains. Dead Union soldiers were buried in the lawn. All of the trees had been cut down for fuel. The Lacys returned to their sad home but were unable to keep it up, and the family sold the home in 1872.

For the next fifty years, a number of different people lived in Chatham Manor. The house was finally restored when Daniel and Helen Devore purchased the home in the 1920s. John Lee Pratt bought Chatham Manor from the Devore family in 1931 and deeded it to the National Park Service in 1975. Today, visitors can stroll the beautiful mansion, where they can learn of its fascinating history and its ghost stories.

Chatham Manor is haunted by the ghost of an English girl who was brought to the colonies by her father to break up a love affair she was having with an English drysalter. Her beau followed her to Chatham Manor, where he secretly renewed their romance. After a few months, they decided to get married, although they knew a formal wedding was out of the question. On the night the couple decided to elope, the young man placed a ladder against the wall of Chatham Manor so that she could exit the house through her bedroom window. When she reached the ground, she was surprised to see George Washington, who had been alerted to the pair's elopement plans by the servants. Washington arrested her lover, and the girl was taken back to England by her father.

The girl eventually married a suitor her father had deemed suitable for her, but she never forgot her lost love. On her deathbed, she vowed to walk her favorite path at Chatham Manor on the anniversary of her death. Many people claim to have seen the girl's mournful spirit on what has come to be known as the "Ghost Walk." Tour guide Lorna Cotner said that she encountered the ghost twice. In November 2006, she detected the unmistakable fragrance of flowers, even though no flowers were in bloom. A few months later, in June 2007, she saw a plume of white smoke outside in the darkness. The English girl's name has been lost, but her memory is kept alive through the frequent ghost sightings at Chatham Manor.

CHARLOTTESVILLE

Castle Hill Manor

In 1764, Thomas Walker built Castle Hill Manor on land he acquired when he married Mildred Meriwether in 1741. Walker played host to a number of famous Americans, including Thomas Jefferson and George Washington. The next two owners of the mansion were the Walkers' youngest son, Francis Walker, and their granddaughter, Judith Page Walker, who married Senator William Cabell Rives. Their son, Colonel Alfred Landon Rives, was chief engineer under General Robert E. Lee during the Civil War. He inherited the mansion. After he died in 1903, his wife, Catherine, and their daughter, Amelie, took control of the estate. Amelie inherited the estate after her mother died in 1909. Amelie became a talented artist and novelist. In fact, three of her novels are set at Castle Hill Manor. Amelie died in 1945 and is buried on the grounds. Today, Castle Hill is a privately owned home in the Keswick Hunt Club District.

Most of the paranormal activity in the old mansion has taken place in the pink bedroom in one of the suites on the ground floor. Amelie Rives said that on several occasions, she smelled perfume that definitely was not hers. Guests sleeping in the bedroom reported being awakened during the night by the sound of disembodied footsteps and other strange noises. Visitors who have seen the ghost describe her as an attractive young woman who annoys people she does not like. One of the guests whom the ghost did not seem to care for was the writer Julien Green, who was so frightened after spending the night in the pink bedroom that he left soon after he woke up. Author Hans Holzer believes that the female ghost is the spirit of one of the women who lived in the house during the Revolutionary War.

HAMPTON

Fort Monroe

The construction of Fort Monroe began in 1819 under the supervision of a French military engineer named Simon Bernard. Slaves and convicts did most of the work on the fort, and it was completed fifteen years later at a cost of $2 million. The sixty-three-acre fort is enclosed by a wall 1.3 miles in circumference. The moat, which is between three and five feet deep, is fed from Mill Creek. The walls are ten feet thick. The casemates were used for defense, living quarters and a prison. After the Civil War, Jefferson Davis was incarcerated in one of these casemate cells. Ironically, Robert E. Lee had been stationed here when he was twenty-four years old. Abraham Lincoln inspected the ironclad *Monitor* during his visit to the fort. Throughout the Civil War, the fort remained under Union control. Over ten thousand newly emancipated slaves lived in the area surrounding Fort Monroe under the provisions of the contraband policies. They referred to Fort Monroe as "Freedom Fort." The old fort was decommissioned on September 15, 2011. On November 1, 2011, President Barrack Obama designated portions of the fort as a National Monument. Today, Fort Monroe is one of the best-preserved—and one of the most haunted—masonry forts in the United States.

At least three of the ghosts haunting the fort have been identified. Jefferson Davis's ghost has been seen walking the ramparts in the evening, just as he did when he was held prisoner there. Quarters No. 1 is haunted by the ghost of Abraham Lincoln, who stayed there during his visit to the fort. The ghost of Edgar Allan Poe, who served for a brief time as sergeant of the artillery, has been sighted in different parts of the fort.

Most of the paranormal activity in Fort Monroe is caused by spirits whose identities have not yet been determined. In Quarters No. 1, paranormal investigators recorded the voice of a little girl calling for her cat, Greta. In the casemates, the group recorded the ghostly sounds of horses' hooves and disembodied voices. Heather McCann, deputy of public affairs at Fort Monroe, was conducting a late-night tour of the fort when she was touched by an invisible arm.

Probably the best known of the Fort Monroe ghost stories is the tale of the White Lady. A young woman who had married a very uptight officer fell in love with a dashing young soldier. One night, while her husband was away, she invited her new love to her bed. They were in the throes of love when the woman's husband burst into the bedroom and shot her. The woman's ghost has been seen many times on the boardwalk, looking for her handsome soldier. All of the witnesses describe her dress as a white nightgown.

MAX MEADOWS

Major Graham Mansion

The Major Graham Mansion was built by his father, Squire David, in the 1830s. Squire and his family lived in what is now the rear frame section of the mansion. Major Graham continued living here after he inherited the property. Major Graham, who was born in 1838, made a fortune on his twelve iron furnaces and forges. He also devoted his time to purchasing a mill and several mines and to completing the mansion. In the 1850s, a local architect from Max Meadows erected the brick additions. In 1989, Josiah Cephas Weaver purchased the mansion. Over the years, the paranormal groups that investigated the mansion have confirmed its reputation as a genuine haunted house.

Several ghosts are said to haunt the Major Graham Mansion. One of these spirits is the ghost of a little girl who lost her parents during the Civil War. She is rumored to have died of tuberculosis in the house. Supposedly, the child's body was kept in a closet until she could be buried outside. The ghost of Major Graham's wife, Martha Bell Pierce, is also said to be an active presence in the house. Legend has it that after Martha went insane, her husband locked her up inside the bedroom now known as Martha's Room. One can still see the date—February 24, 1864—that she etched on the window with her diamond ring. A third ghost is the spirit of a crying bride whose image has been seen staring out of one of the upstairs bedroom windows.

Even the land itself is reputed to be haunted. The Major Graham House was built on the site of a log cabin owned by Joseph Baker. One night in 1796, Baker was murdered by two of his slaves, Bob and Sam. The slaves were apprehended and hanged from a hickory tree standing on a hill. The pair had been forced to dig their own graves before the hanging. The ghosts of the slaves still roam the property, looking for justice.

The Virginia Paranormal Society has investigated the Major Graham Mansion several times since 2006. One of the investigators has felt a hand pulling his hair and tugging on his pants while on the second floor. All of the members heard ghostly voices in a room upstairs when they were the only ones in the house. Down through the years, the group has recorded fifteen Class A EVPs. The voice was easily understandable, and it did not need amplification. The ghosts of the Major Graham Mansion are trying to make verbal contact with the living.

MOUNT VERNON

Woodlawn Plantation

George Washington had no children, but he did raise his wife Martha's two daughters from a previous marriage, Patsy and Jackie. Jackie married young and had four children. Her youngest child, Eleanor, was only four and a half months old when her mother died. George and Martha took in "Nelly," as Eleanor was known, and another sibling and raised them at Mount Vernon.

George Washington was immensely pleased when Nelly grew up and married his nephew, Major Lawrence Lewis. Washington gave them two thousand acres of land overlooking Mount Vernon and hired an architect, D. William Thornton, to design their home, which was completed between 1800 and 1805. The couple had eight children, only three of whom survived to adulthood. After Nelly's husband died in 1839, she moved to her son's house. However, her descendants continued to live at Woodlawn Plantation until 1846.

Woodlawn Plantation, Mount Vernon, Virginia. *Courtesy of the Library of Congress.*

Woodlawn Plantation had a number of different owners over the next fifty years. In 1896, Woodlawn was so severely damaged by a hurricane that it was abandoned for six years. The fine old home was extensively renovated in the twentieth century when the National Trust for Historic Places purchased it. Today, Woodlawn Plantation is open to the general public.

Woodlawn Plantation is now home to a number of ghosts that manifest themselves in a variety of ways. Candles that are extinguished are found relit a few minutes later. Doors are said to lock themselves and to slam shut inexplicably. Pictures on walls and items on shelves fall to the floor for no apparent reason. The door of an antique armoire opens on its own, lights go off and on and visitors have felt someone tap them on the shoulders when they are alone in the master bedroom.

Some of these spirits have personalities. The ghost of a little girl about six years old has been seen on the back staircase to the second floor. Men wearing the fashions of the eighteenth century have been reported walking around the house. The ghost of George Washington is said to ride around the house on a white horse.

The plantation's most famous paranormal event occurred in the 1930s in the Lafayette Room. A woman laid her baby in the crib and left the room. When she heard the baby crying a few minutes later, she ran back into the room. She was shocked to find the infant lying on top of the dresser. Some people familiar with the history of the house believe that this could be the ghost of Agnes Lewis, who died in the house in 1820, when she was fifteen years old. She is also said to move furniture around in the room. Agnes could be the ghost that was seen staring out the bedroom window in 1992.

WORKS CITED

Books

Brown, Alan. *Haunted Pensacola*. Charleston, SC: The History Press, 2010.

Coleman, Elaine. *Texas Haunted Forts*. Plano: Republic of Texas Press, 2001.

Davidson, Michelle. *Florida's Haunted Hospitality*. Atglen, PA: Schiffer Publishing, 2013.

DeBolt, Margaret Wayt. *Savannah Spectres and Other Strange Tales*. Virginia Beach, VA: Donning Company Publishers, 2000.

Domine, David. *Phantoms of Old Louisville*. Kuttawa, KY: McClanahan Publishing House, 2006.

Dwyer, Jeff. *Ghost Hunter's Guide to New Orleans*. Gretna, LA: Pelican Publishing Company, Inc., 2010.

Easley, Nicole Carlson. *Hauntings in Florida's Panhandle*. Atglen, PA: Schiffer, 2009.

Haskins, Lola. *Fifteen Florida Cemeteries*. Tallahassee: University Press of Florida, 2011.

Hauck, Dennis William. *Haunted Places: The National Directory*. New York: Penguin, 1996.

Jenkins, Greg. *Florida's Ghostly Legends and Haunted Florida*. Sarasota, FL: Pineapple Press, 2007.

Johnson, Sandra, and Leora Sutton. *Ghosts, Legends and Folklore of Old Pensacola*. Pensacola, FL: Pensacola Historical Society, 1990.

Jones, Ray. *Haunted Lighthouses*. Guilford, CT: Globe Pequot Press, 2010.

Klein, Victor. *New Orleans Ghosts*. Metairie, LA: Lycanthrope Press, 1993.
————. *New Orleans Ghosts II*. Metairie, LA: Lycanthrope Press, 1999.
————. *New Orleans Ghosts III*. Metairie, LA: Lycanthrope Press, 2004.
Lapham, Dave. *Ancient City Hauntings: More Ghosts of St. Augustine*. Sarasota, FL: Pineapple Press, 2004.
Lewis, Chad, and Terry Fisk. *The Florida Road Guide to Haunted Locations*. Eau Claire, WI: Unexplained Research Publishing Company, 2010.
Montz, Larry, and Daena Smoller. *ISPR Investigates the Ghosts of New Orleans*. Atglen, PA: Whitford Press, 2000.
Moore, Joyce Elson. *Haunt Hunter's Guide to Florida*. Sarasota, FL: Pineapple Press, 1998.
Norman, Michael, and Beth Scott. *Historic Haunted America*. New York: TOR, 1995.
Parker, Elizabeth. *Mobile Ghosts: Alabama's Haunted Port City*. Mobile, AL: Apparition Publishing, 2001.
————. *Mobile Ghosts II: The Waterline*. Mobile, AL: Apparition Publishing, 2004.
Powell, Jack. *Haunting Sunshine*. Sarasota, FL: Pineapple Press, 2001.
Reeser, Tim. *Ghost Stories of Tampa, Florida*. St. Petersburg, FL: 1stSight Press, 2007.
Saxton, Lyle. *Gumbo Ya-Ya: Folk Tales of Louisiana*. Gretna, LA: Pelican Publishing Company, Inc., 1991.
Sillery, Barbara. *The Haunting of Louisiana*. Gretna, LA: Pelican Publishing Company, Inc., 2001.
Taylor, Troy. *The Ghost Hunter's Handbook*. Alton, IL: Whitechapel Press, 2001.
————. *Haunted New Orleans*. Alton, IL: Whitechapel Press, 2000.
Thompson, James West. *Beauvoir: A Walk through History*. Biloxi, MS: Beauvoir Press, 2005.
Windham, Kathryn Tucker. *Jeffrey's Latest 13*. Tuscaloosa: University of Alabama Press, 1982.
Winer, Richard, and Nancy Osborn. *Haunted Houses*. New York: Bantam, 1979.

Websites

Abbott, Jim. "'Florida's Greatest Rainy-Day Attraction!" http://www.orlandosentinel.com/travel/destinations/centralflorida/orl-travel-abbott-101809.
Adams County, MS Genealogical and Historical Research. "Natchez City Cemetery: Adams Count, MS." www.natchezbelle.org/adams-ind/nec2.htm.

Adcock, Andrea, and Robert Cleveland. "Did Hurricane Katrina Scare the Spooks Away from the Big Easy?" http://www.mysterious-america.net/bigeasyghosts.html.

Amandolare, Sarah. "Haunted New Orleans." http://www.findingdulcinea.com/features/feature-articles/2008/october/Haunted-New-Orle...

Angelsghosts.com. "Ghost Tours of the Southern US." http://angelsghosts.com/ghost_tours_south.html.

Antoines.com. "Antoine Restaurant." http://www.antoines.com/history.html.

Apowell.hubpages.com. "The Ghosts of the USS *Alabama*." http://apowell.hubpages.com/hub/The-Ghosts-of-the-USS-Alabama.

Arkansas Historic Preservation Program. "Mayberry Springs, Crystal Springs, Garland County." http://www.arkansaspreservation.com/historic-properties/_search_nomination_popup.aspx...

Arnaudsrestaurant.com. "About Arnaud's Restaurant." http://www.arnaudsrestaurant.com/about.

———. "Ghost Stories." http://www.arnaudsrestaurant.com/about/ghost-stories.

———. "Happy Halloween." http://www.arnaudsrestaurant.com/ar/2011/a-little-history/happy-halloween.

Battleship USS *Alabama*. "The History of the USS Alabama (BB 60)." http://www.ussalabama.com/history.php.

Beauvoir.org. "History of Beauvoir." http://beauvoir.org/history.html.

Boonetavernhotel.com. "An Historic Berea Hotel." http://www.boonetavernhotel.com/about/history.

Bourbonorleans.com. "Bourbon Orleans Hotel." http://www.bourbonorleans.com/history.

Branning, Debe. "Arizona Ghost Hunter Travels: New Moon and Vampires at the Old Ursuline Convent." http://www.examiner.com/arizona-haunted-sites-in-phoenix/arizona-ghost-hunter-travels-...

Broome, Fiona. "About 'Ghost Hunters' aka the TAPS guys." http://www.hollowhill.com/ghost-hunting/TAPS.htm.

Bryant, Charles, and Jessika Toothman. "Top 10 Hotels That Will Scare the Daylights out of You." http://science.howstuffworks.com/science-vs-myth/afterlife/top-5-hauntedhotels1.htm.

Cafev.com. "Lafayette's First Inn." http://www.cafev.com/history.html.

Capo, Bill. "Investigating Some of New Orleans' Most Haunted Museums." http://www.wwltv.com/news/Ghosts-In-The-Museums-132272383.html.

Central Rappahannock Regional Library. "The Ghosts of Fredericksburg." http://www.librarypoint.org/the_ghosts_of_fredericksburg.

Ceprofs.civil.tamu.edu. "Approach and Storm." https://ceprofs.civil.tamu.edu/llowery/personal/songs/hurricane/thestorm/approach.htm.

Cheri, Cecile. "Secret Enclaves of New Orleans and Quaint Hotels You've Never Heard Of." http://voices.yahoo.com/secret-enclaves-orleans-quaint-hotels-youve-6319616.html?cat=16.

Cherokeegold.net. "The Legend of Trahlyta." http://www.cherokeegold.net/stonepilegap.html.

Chretienpoint.com. "Chretien Point Plantation History." http://www.chretienpoint.com/Lafayette/history.html.

Coastalbreeznews.com. "The Legend of the Pirate Gasparilla." http://www.coastalbreezenews.com/2010/03/26/the-legend-of-the-pirate-gasparilla.

Coastal Georgia Historical Society. "St. Simons Lighthouse History." http://www.saintsdimonslighthouse.org/lhh.html.

Contactmusic.com. "Nicholas Cage—Cage Spooked by Haunted Home." http://www.contactmusic.com/news/cage-spooked-by-haunted-home-1079309.

Cornstalkhotel.com. "The Cornstalk Hotel." http://www.cornstalkhotel.com/our_history.html.

Cox, Dale. "The Ghost of the St. Simons Lighthouse—St. Simons Island, Georgia." http://wwww.exploresouthernhistory.com/gastsimons2.html.

Crystalbeach.com. "Point Bolivar Lighthouse on Bolivar Peninsula, Texas." http://www.crystalbeach.com/light.htm.

Danahy, Barbara. "Murder at the Sultan's Palace." http://www.nola.com/haunted/harem/hauntings/murder.html.

Dauphineorleans.com. "Dauphine Orleans." http://www.dauphineorleans.com/packages.stml.

Dauphine Orleans Hotel. "History." http://dauphineorleans-px.trvclick.com/history.html.

Dauphinislandhistory.org. "Historic Fort Gaines on Dauphin Island, Alabama." http://www.dauphinislandhistory.org/ft_gainers/ftgaines_pandb.htm.

Dauphinisland.org. "Historic Fort Gaines." http://www.dauphinisland.org/fort.htm.

Dixit, Rachana. "A Ghost at Chatham?" http://fredericksburg.com/News/FLS/2007/062007/06232007/294672.

Dupontmansion.com. "DuPont Mansion Bed and Breakfast Inn." http://www.dupontmansion.com/history.

Edwards, Jennifer. "Local Historian Tells Stories from Natchez City Cemetery in New Book." www.natchezdmocrat.com/news/2009/now/04local-historian-tells-stories-natchez.

Egmont Key Lighthouse. "Egmont Key Lighthouse and More." http://www.egmontkey-lighthouse.com.

Encyclopedia of Alabama. "History Museum of Mobile." http://encyclopediaofalabama.org/face/Article.jsp?id=-3047.

———. "New Orleans and Its Ghosts." http://www.essortment.com/new-orleans-its-ghosts-42562.html.

———. "University of South Alabama (USA)." http://www.encyclopediaofalabama.org/face/Article.jsp?id=h-1646.

Examiner.com. "The phantom Reverends of Old Christ Church." http://www.examiner.com//x-45527-Fort-Lauderdale-Paranormal-Examiner-y2010m5d20-T…

Experience New Orleans! "Halloween, Ghosts and Voodoo." http://www.experienceneworleans.com/halloween.html.

Exploresouthernhistory.com. "Beauvoir, Home of Jefferson Davis." http://www.explore-southernhistory.com/Beauvoir.

———. Beauvoir in Biloxi, Mississippi—Final Home of President Jefferson Davis." http://southernhistory.blogspot.com/2012/02/beauvoir-in-biloxi-mississippi-final.html.

Faber, Dustin. "Return Visits to Haunted Cemetery Explains Phenomenon." http://www.asuherald.com/2.11408/return-visits-to-haunted-cemetery-explains-phenomeno...

Fabuloustravel.com. "The Ghost of Café Vermilionville." http://www.faculoustravel.com/usa/articles/391/21887.

Film North Florida. "East Hill: Tower East: Old Sacred Heart Hospital." http:filmnorthflorida.com/photos/location/East-Hill:-Tower-East:-Old-Sacred-Heart-Hosp…

Findarticles.com. "The Haunting of the Light." http://findarticles.com/p/articles/mi_mOPRY/is_6_2007/ai_n25488687.

Flickr. "The Knott House." http://www.flickr.com/photos/freestone/149251586.

ForgottenUSA. "Tallassee—The Lively Building." http://forgottenusa.com/haunts/FL/4858/The%20Lively%Building.

Fortdesoto.com. "Fort De Soto Park." http://www.fortdesoto.com/fortconstruction.php.

Fort Zachary Taylor State Park. "History." http://www.fortzacharytaylor.com/history.html.

Franco, Virginia. "Where Monroe's Blakeney House is Concerned…it Depends on Whom You Talk To." http://www.unioncountyweekly.com/news/2011/10/haunted-or-not.

Frenchquarterinns.com. "Hotel St. Pierre." http://wwew.frenchquarterinns. com/hotelspierre/history.html.

Galiano, Amanda. "The Ghosts of Arkansas." http://littlerock.about.com/ cs/urbanlegends/a/aaghosts_2.htm.

Garden & Gun. "The Temptress of Castle Hill." http://gardenandgun. com/article/temptress-castle-hill.

Gautierpride.com. "History of Gautier." http://www.gautierpride.com/ history.htm.

———. "Singing River Legend." http://gautierpride.org/Singing_River_ Legend.html.

Ghastlygirl.com. "Princess Hall." http://ghastlygirl.com/haunted-directory/arkansas/princess-hall-university-of-arkansas-bee...

Ghosteyes.com. "The Hauntings of the Provincial Hotel." http://www. ghosteyes.com/hauntings-provincial-hotel.

———. "Most Haunted Place in America: Garden of Hope Cemetery." http://www.ghosteyes.com/haunted-garden-hope-cemetery.

———. "Most Haunted Places in America: The Royalty Theater." http:// www.ghosteyes.com/captain-royalty-theater.

———. "Most Haunted Places in America: Saint Louis Cemetery No. 1." http://www.Ghosteyes.com/ghosts-st-louis-cemetery-1.

Ghostinmysuitcase.com. "Stories from Natchez City Cemetery." www. ghostinmysuitcase.com/places/natchez/index.htm.

Ghosts and Ghouls. "The Ghosts of Savannah's Bonaventure Cemetery." http://ghostsnghouls.com/2012/11/25/haunted-bonaventure-cemetery.

Ghosts of America. "Gulf Shores, Alabama Ghost Sightings." http://www. ghostofamerica.com/3/Alabama_Gulf_Shores_ghost_sightings.html.

Ghost Stories and Haunted Places. "The Ghosts of the USS *Alabama*." http://ghoststoriesandhauntedplaces.blogspot.com/2010/09/ghosts-of-uss-alabama.html.

Ghosttowns.com. "Fort Pickens." http://www.ghosttowns.com/states/fl/ fortpickens.html.

Goodwood Museum. "History." http://www.goodwoodmuseum.org/ history.php.

Granato, Sheri. "Haunted America: The Ghosts of the Major Graham Mansion in Max Meadows, Virginia." http://voices.yahoo.com/ haunted-america-ghosts-major-graham-mansion-11482060.html?c...

———. "Haunted America: The Ghosts of the Martha Washington Hotel and Spa in Abingdon, Virginia." http://voices.yahoo.com/haunted-america-ghosts-martha-washington-11921803.html?cat=37.

Graveaddiction.com. "Muriel's Restaurant." http://www.graveaddiction. com/Muriel.html.

GulfBase.org."Deer Island." http://www.gulgbase.org/reef/view. php?rid=deer1.

Gulf Shores, Alabama. "Ft. Pickens near Pensacola, FL." http://www.gulf-shores-alabama.net/ft-pickens.html.

———. "Halloween Ghost Pictures." http://halloweensunseen.com/ faceutmb.html.

Hames, Jacqueline. "The Haunting of Fort Monroe." http://www.army. mil/article/27724/The_haunting_of_Fort_Monroe.

Hampton.gov. "Fort Monroe." http://www.hampton.gov/index. aspx?NID=1912.

Harding University. "Harding: History." http://www.harding.edu/about/ history.

HauntedAccommodations.com. "Haunted Key West." http://www. hauntedaccom-modations.com/hauntedkeywest.htm.

Haunted America Tours. "Mississippi Haunted Gulf Coast." Http:// www.hauntedameri-catours.com/hauntedstates/hauntedmississippi/ mississippigulfcoast…

Hauntedhouses.com. "Castle Hill Manor." http://www.hauntedhouses. com/states/va/castle_hill_manor.htm.

———. "DuPont Mansion." http://www.hauntedhouses.com/states/ky/ dupont_mansion.htm.

———."Fort Gaines—HauntedHouses.com." http://www.hauntedhouses. com/states/al/fort_gaines.htm.

———."Fort Pulanski." http://www.hauntedhouses.com/states/ga/fort_ pulaski.htm.

———. "Hermann-Grima House." http://www.hauntedhouses.com/ states/la/herman_grima_house.htm.

———. "Saint Louis Cemetery." www.hauntedhouses.com/states/la/ saint_louis_cemetery.htm.

Hauntedhovel.com. "The Columns Hotel, New Orleans." http://www. Hauntedhovel.com/thecolumnshotel.html.

———. "The Cornstalk Hotel, New Orleans." http://www.hauntedhovel. com/cornstalkhotel.html.

———. "The Old Lighthouse, St. Simons Island." http://hauntedhovel. com/oldlighthouse.html.

———. "St. Louis Cathedral, New Orleans." http://www.hauntedhovel. com/stlouiscathedral.html.

Haunted New Orleans Tours. "Brennan's Restaurant Ghosts." http://www. hauntedneworleanstours.com/buildings/BRENNANS.

———. "Griffin House." http://www.hauntedneworleans.com/ hauntedhouses/GriffinHouse.

———. "Haunted New Orleans Top Ten Haunted Hotels." http://www. haunted neworleanstours.com/toptenhaunted/toptenhauntednolahotels.

———. "New Orleans French Opera House Ghost." http:// hauntedneworleanstours.com/frenchoperahouse.

———. "St. Louis Cathedral Hauntings, and a Touch of Ghostly History." http://www.neworleanstours.com/hauntedstlouiscathedral.

———. "The Sultan's House: The Gardette-Laprete House." http://www. hauntedneworleans tours. com/hauntedhouses/TheSultansGhost.

———. "Top Ten Haunted Houses." http://www.hauntedneworleanstours. com/toptenhaunted/toptenhauntedneworleanshouses.

———. "Top Ten Haunted Restaurants." http://www.hauntedneworleanstours. com/toptenhaunted/toptenhauntedresturantsnola.

———. "Top Ten Most Haunted New Orleans Locations." http://www.hauntedneworleanstours.com/toptenhaunted/ toptenhauntedNewOrleanslocations.

Haunted North Carolina. "Devil's Tramping Ground." http://www. hauntednc.com/legends/devil-s-tramping-ground.html.

———. "The Haunted Provincial Hotel in New Orleans." http://www. haunted-places-to-gp.com/provincial-hotel.html.

———. "Haunted Ships: The USS *Lexington* in Corpus Christi, Texas." http://www.haunted-places-to-go.com/haunted-ships-1.html.

Hauntedstories.net. "Devil's Tramping Ground." http://hauntedstories. net/devil-stories/north-carolina/devils-tramping-ground.

———. "The Haunting of Biltmore." http://hauntedstories.net/haunted-houses/north-carolina/haunting-biltmore.

Hauntedva.blogspot.com. "The Haunted Commonwealth." http:// hauntedva.blogspot.com/2010/11/fort-monroe-hapton-va.html.

Hauntsofamerica.blogspot.com. "The Haunting of Fort Gaines." http:// hauntsofamerica.blogspot.com/2007/08/haunting-of-fort-gaines.html.

Historical Truth 101. "The Richards DAR House Museum Mobile Alabama." http://www.historicaltruth101.com/public/The_Richards_ DAR_House_Museum_Mobile_...

History Museum of Mobile. "Other Locations." http://www. museumofmobile.com/other_locs.phn.

HMdb.org. "Landes-McDonough House." http://www.hmdb.org/Marker=50048.

Hsnp.com. "Mayberry Springs Inn, 1895." http://www.hsnp.com/zz_mayberry_springs_inn.htm.

Hubpages.com. "Ghosts of New Orleans." http://jy3402.hubpages.com/hub/Ghosts-of-New-Orleans.

Insanejournal.com. "Bienwenue a Mercier Plantation." http://lesrevenants.insanejournal.com/425.html.

Jeong, John. "Mayberry Inn: Hot Springs, Arkansas." http://hauntedplacesofusa.blogspot.com/2009/10/mayberry-inn-hot-springs-arkansas.html.

Jungleprada. "Welcome to Sacred Lands." http://www.jungleprada.blogspot.com.

Keating, Sharon. "Great New Orleans Ghost Stories and Hauntings." http://gonewrleans.about.com/od/ghostandhauntings/a/new-orleans-ghost-stories.htm.

———. "Haunted in New Orleans." http://goneworleans.about.com/od/famouslandmarks/a/hauntedno.htm.

———. "Top New Orleans Haunted Hotels." http://goneworleans.about.com/od/hotels/tp/hauntedhotels.htm.

Kramer, Jillian. "Alarm Panel Mysteriously Indicates Fire 40 Years after Power Cut Off." http://blog.al.com/live/2010/08/post_78.html.

Lalouisiane.com. "La Louisiane Bar & Bistro." http://www.lalouisiane.com/history.html.

Lanauxmansion.com. "The Lanaux Mansion." http://www.lanauxmansion.com/aboutlanaux.html.

Legendexplorers.topic-board.com. "Garden of Hope Cemetery." http://legendexplorers.Topic-board.com/t336-garden-of-hope-cemetery-gautier-ms.

Lepavillon.com. "Le Pavilion Hotel." http://www.lepavillon.com/history.htm.

Lighthousefriends.com. "Bolivar Point, TX." http://www.lighthousefriends.com/light.asp?ID=152.

———. "Pensacola, FL." http://www.lighthousefriends.com/light.asp?ID=589.

———. "Saint Simons, GA." http://www.lighthousefriends.com/light.asp?ID=3

Lodging.uptake.com. "Five Haunted Hotels in New Orleans." http://lodging.uptake.com/blog/five-haunted-hotels-in-new-orleans.html.

Lynn, Newt. "Jackson Barracks." http://www.myneworleans.com/Louisiana-Life/March-April-2010/Jackson-Barracks.

Mack, Patricia. "Haunted Restaurant." http://www.gayot.com/blog/haunted-restaurants-ghost-stories-sightings-muriels-jackson-sq…

Majorgrahammansion.com. "Mansion History." http://majorgrahammansion. com/history-mansion-ours-and-new-graham-ghosts-graves-gh...

Mamalakis, Mario. "Lafayette's First Inn." http://www.cafev.com/history.html.

Marin, Patricia. "Virginia Paranormal Society Discovers Ghostly Activities at Major Graham's Mansion." http://www.examiner.com/article/ virginia-paranormal-society-discovers-ghostly-activities...

Masyk-Jackson, Janis. "The Most Haunted Hotels in New Orleans." http:// suite101.com/article/the-most-haunted-hotels-=in-new-orleans-a20712.

Memphis-Mid South Ghost Hunters. "Ghost Webcams." http://www. memphisghost-Hunters.com/ghost_webcams.html.

Merwin, Laura. "Ghost Hunters Miss the Mark in 'French Quarter Phantoms' at the U.S. Mint." http://www.masslive.com/television/ index.ssf/2011/03/ghost_hunters_miss_the_mark_in...

Militaryghosts.com. "Fort Pulaski." http://www.militaryghosts.com/ pulaski.html.

Mississippi Department of Marine Resources. "Deer Island Preserve." http://www.dmr.ms.gov/Mississippi-gems/211-deer-island.

Mitchell Historic Properties. "Galveston's 'Haunted' Hotel Galvez Offers October Mobile Ghosts. Ghost-oberfest, Day Three." http:// mobileghosts.net/2010/10/03/ghost-oberfest-day-3.

———. "Ghost-oberfest, Day 24: Haunted Saraland." http://mobileghosts. net/2010/10/24/ghost-oberfest-day-24-haunted-saraland.

Monroe County Health Department Florida. "Epidemiology." http://www. keyshealth.com/HealthServices/EPI/Index.html.

Muriels.com. "Muriel's." http://www.muriels.com/html/ghost.html.

Mystic-places.blogspot.com. "Biloxi." http://mystic-places.blogspot,com/2007/06/ Biloxi.html.

Natchezcitycemetery.com. "Welcome to the Natchez City Cemetery." www. natchezcitycemetery.com/custom/webpage.cfm?content=content&id=2.

National Park Service. "Fort Pickens." http://www.nps.gov/guis/ planyourvisit/fort-pickens.htm.

Ncvacationcabin.com. "Appalachian State University Ghost Story." http:// www.ncvacationcabin.com/article.php?mode=search&article=60.

Needhambryanchapterdar.com. "The Richards DAR House." http:// needhambryanchapterdar.com/project_richardshouse.htm.

Newsorleansghosts.com. "Haunted New Orleans." http://www. neworleansghosts.com/haunted _new_orleans.htm.

Neworleansonline.com. "Old U.S. Mint." http://www.neworleansonline. com/directory/location.php?locationID=1277.

Noble Manor. "About the Inn." http://www.noblemanor.com/about-inn.

Nolacom. "Armory Ghost Story Lingers." http://www.nola.com/haunted/ ghosts/armory.html.

———. "History of the Sultan's Palace." http://www.nola.com/haunted/ index.ssf/hauntings/ history_of_the_sultans_palace.html.

North Carolina Ghost Stories and Legends. "The Chimney Rock Apparitions." http://www.northcarolinaghosts.com/mountains/chimney-rock-apparitions.php.

———. "The Devil's Tramping Ground." http://www.northcarolinaghosts. com/piedmont/devils-tramping-ground.php.

———. "The Ghost of Chicken Alley." http://www.northcarolinaghosts. com/mountains/ghost-chicken-alley.php.

———. "Ghost of East Hall." http://www.northcarolinaghossts.com/ mountains/ghost-east-hall.php.

———. "Ghosts of the Biltmore House." http://www.northcarolinaghosts. com/mountains/biltmore-house-ghosts.php.

Ocala.com. "Attorney Opens Law Office in Seven Sisters Inn." http://www. ocala.com/Article/20110/ARTICLES/100109823.

———. "'Ghost Hunters' Drawn to Ocala Inn." http://www.ocala.com/ article/20080930/NEWS/809290364.

Oldtownmanor.com. "Old Town Manor." http://www.oldtownmanor. com/index.shtml.

Omnihotels.com. "The Omni Royal Orleans Hotel—Haunted Tales." http:// www.omni-Hotels.com/ExclusiveOffers/HauntedTravelsRoyalOrleans. aspx.

Paranormalknowledge.com. "Chretien Point Plantation." http://www. paranormalknowledge.com/articles/chretien-point-plantation.html.

———. "Hotel St. Pierre." http://www.paranormalknowledge.com/ articles/hotel-st-pierre-html.

———. "Jackson Barracks Military Museum." http://www. paranormalknowledge.com/articles/Jackson-barracks-military-museum.html.

———. "Muriel's Jackson Square." http://www.paranormalknowledge. com/articles/muriels-jackson-square.html.

———. "Napoleon House." http://www.paranormalknowledge.com/ articles/napoleon-house.html.

———. "The Old Ursuline Convent." http://www.paranormalknowledge. com/articles/the-old-ursuline-convent.html.

———. "The Old U.S. Mint." http://www.paranormalknowledge.com/ articles/the-old-us-mint.html.

Paranormalstories.blogspot.com. "Woodland Plantation." http://paranormalstories.blogspot.com/2009/06/woodland-plantation.html.

Phantoms & Monsters. "Unexplained Lights at Mobile, Alabama Fire Station." http://naturalplane.blogspot.com/2010/08/unexplained-lights-at-mobile-alabama.html.

Prairieghosts.com. "Haunted Arkansas: The Old State House." http://www.prairieghosts.com/oldstat.htm.

Project Ghost Find. "East Residence Hall, Appalachian State University, Boone, NC." http://www.freewebs.com/ghostfind818/investigationsstories.htm.

Realhaunts.com. "USS Alabama BB-60." http://www.realhaunts.com/united-states/uss-alabama-bb-60.

Reich, Holly. "Hotel Provincial." http://honeymoons.about.com/od/neworleans/ss/princial_2.htm.

Remembercliffside.com. "Oddities of the Chimney Rock Gorge." http://remembercliffside.com/history/the_county/oddities.html.

Richardson, Joy. "New Orleans' Café Lafitte Haunted by Two Literary Greats." http://suite101.com/article/new-oreleans-cafe-lafitte-haunted-by-two-literary-greats-a260544.

Roadsidegeorgia.com. "Stonepile Gap." http://roadsidegeorgia.com/site/stonepile.html.

Rootsweb.ancestry.com. "Blakeney-L Archives." http://archiver.rootsweb.ancestry.com/th/read/BLAKENEY/2003-11/1068041625.

———. "Kenilworth Plantation Home: A Little History." http://archiver.rootsweb.ancestry.com/th/read/LA-LGHS/2005-10/1129427671.

Roussos, Nicholas. "Cry Baby Bridge." http://www.nicholasroussos.com/general/cry-baby-bridge.

Safetyharborspa.com. "Resort History." www.safetyharborspa.com/history/history.html.

Sanders, Bryan, and Scott Wooten. "The Light at Keller's Chapel." http://johnnyd130.tripod.com/id2.html.

Sanfranciscoplantation.org. "San Francisco Plantation." http://www.sanfranciscoplantation.org/history.asp.

Scaryforkids.com. "USS Lexington." http://wwww.scaryforkids.com/uss-lexington/seefloridaonline.com/oldesthouse.

Seeks Ghosts. "The Ghost of Calloway." http://seeksghosts.blogspot.com/2011/09/ghost-of-galloway.html.

———. "Haunted Springer Opera House." http://seeksghosts.blogspot.com/2012/03/htuned-springer-opera-house.html.

———. "Virginia's Woodlawn Plantation." http://seeksghosts.blogspot. com/2014/virginia-woodlawn-plantation.html.

Shoestringweekends.wordpress.com. "One of America's Most Haunted Rooms!" http://shoestringweekends.wordpress.com/2010/12/19/ haunted-room.

Southern Area Paranormal Society. "The Rock & Roll Cemetery-Ocean Springs MS." http://saps-ghosts.blogspot.com/2009/04/rock-roll-cemetery-ocean-springs-ms.html.

Southern Spirit Guide. "'There's a light'—Christ Church, Frederica." http://southernspiritguide.blogspot.com/20122/03/theres-lightchrist-church-frederica.html.

Stefko, Jill. "Haunted Hotel's Provincial's Ghosts." http://suite101.com/ article/haunted-provincials-ghosts-a198202.

———. "Haunted Pascagoula River, Deer Island & Blackman and Waveland Houses." http://suite101.com/article/ghosts-and-legends-of-the-mississippi-gulf-coast-a181418.

Stewart, L.A. "Biltmore Estate in Asheville, North Carolina-Ghosts, Spirits." http://voices.yahoo.com/biltmore-estate-asheville-north-carolina-ghosts-6290840.html?cat...

Stlouiscathedral.org. "History of the St. Louis Cathedral." http:// stlouiscathedral.orb/early_history.html.

Stolznow, Karen. "The Haunted (Pseudo) History of Bonaventure Cemetery." http://www.csicop.org/specialarticles/show/the_haunted_ pseudo+of_bonaventure_c...

Strangegr.tripod.com. "Ghosts: Strange and Paranormal Activity." http:// strangegr.tripod.com/strangeandparanormalactivities./id40html.

Strangeusa.com. "Cretien Point Plantation." http://www.strangeusa.com/ Viewlocation.aspx?id=4545.

———. "U.S.S. Alabama." http://www.strangeusa.com/Viewlocation. aspx?id=63797.

Sullivan, J. Michael. "Countless Number of Ghost Stories, Legends of Old San Patricio Abound." http://www.mysoutex.com/pages/full_story_ landing/push?article-countless+number_of+g…

Thecolumns.com. "The Columns Hotel." http://www.thecolumns.com/ about.htm.

Thecorridors.com. "Haunted: Mobile, Alabama." http://www.thecorridors. com/mobil//eal.html.

Theexpressionist.com. "A Sacred Land." http://www.theexpressionist. com/tag/boca-ciega-bay.

Themoonlitroad.com. "The Sausage Ghost." http://themoonlitroad.com/the-sausage-ghost.

Theplayers.org. "About the Players Theatre." http://theplayers.org/?page_id=356.

Thevanguardonlinecom. "Seaman's Bethel Theatre Getting Renovated, Honors Moving." http://www.thevanguardonline.com/campus/471-honors-moving.html.

Thewhiskeydregs.com. "The Haunted Traveler: The Dauphine Orleans Hotel, New Orleans, LA." http://thewhiskeydregs.com/2010/12/30/the-haunted-trveler-the-dauphine-orleans-hotel-n...

Thewhitenoiseforum.com. "The White Noise Forum." http://www.thewhitenoise-Forum.com/main/view_topic.php?id=2804&forum_id=12.

Toptenz.net. "Top 10 Most Haunted Cities in the U.S." http://www.toptenz.net/Top-10-most-haunted-cities-in-the-u-s.php.

Treasurelore.com. "The Story of Juan Gomez." http://www.treasurelore.com/florida/gasparilla.htm.

Tripod.com. "Mayberry Inn." http://johnnyd130.tripod.com/id2.html.

Unexplainable.net. "Jean Lafitte: Gentleman Pirate." http://www.unexplainable.net/article_15781.shtml.

U-s-history.com "The Temperance Movement." http://www.u-s-history.com/pages/h1054.html.

Voices.yahoo.com. "Island Specters: The Haunting of Dauphin Island, Alabama." http://voices.yahoo.com/island-specters-haunting-dauphin-island-alabama-1989938.html?ca…

WDBJ7.com. "Syfy's 'Ghost Hunters' Investigate Local Haunt." http://articles.wdbj7/cp,2012-02007/ghost-stories-31036037.

Wegoplaces.com. "Chretien Point Plantation." http://www.wegoplaces.com/_1373.aspx.

Wikipedia. "Beauvoir (Biloxi, Mississippi)." http://en.wikipedia.org/wiki/Beauvoir_(Biloxi,_Mississippi).

———. "Bragg-Mitchell Mansion." http://en.wikipedia.oprg/wiki/Bragg-Mitchell_Mansion.

———. "Castle Hill (Virginia)." http://en.wikipedia.org/wiki/Castle_Hill?+Virginia).

———. "Chatham Manor." http://www.nps.gov/frsp/chatham.htm.

———. "Devil's Tramping Ground." http://en.wikipedia.org/wiki/Devil's_Tramping_Ground.

———. "Florida Crackers." http://en.wikipedia.org/wiki/Florida_cracker.

———. "Fort Pickens." http://en.wikipedia.org/wiki/Fort/Pickens.

————. "Gautier, Mississippi." http://en.wikipedia.org/wiki/Gautier,_Mississippi.

————. "Jackson Barracks." http://en.wikipedia.org/wiki/Jackson_Barracks.

————. "Jose Gaspar." http://en.wikipedia.org/wiki/Jos%C3%A9_Gaspar.

————. "Martha Washington Inn." http://en.wikipedia.org/wiki/Martha_Washington_Inn.

————. "New Orleans Mint." http://en.wikipedia.org/wiki/New_Orleans_Mint.

————. "Old State House (Little Rock)." http://en.wikipedia.org/wiki/Old_State_House_(Little_Rock).

————. "Old Ursuline Convent, New Orleans." http://en.wikipedia.org/wiki/Old_Ursuline_Convent,_New_Orleans.

————. "Omni Royal Orleans." http://en.wikipedia.org/wiki/Omni_Royal_Orleans.

————. "Saint Louis Cemetery." http://en.wikipedia.org/wiki/Saint_Louis_Cemetery.

————. "St. Louis Cathedral, New Orleans." Http://en.wikipedia.org/wiki/St._Louis_Cathedral,_New_Orleans.

————. "University of South Alabama." http://en.wikipedia.org/wiki/University_of_South_Alabama.

Wright, Robin. "Cry Baby Bridge & Kali Oka." http://www.realhaunts.com/united-states/cry-baby-bridge..

Yourobserver.com. "The Observer Hunts Ghosts at the Players Theatre." http://www.yourobserver.com/news/Sarasota/Front-Page/1027201114971/The-Observer-hun…

Zubowski, Courtney. "Pro Ghost Hunters Try to Contact Spirits at Historical Hotel Galvez." http://www.khou.com/news/Paranormal-investigators-try-to-contact-ghosts-at-historical-H…

Zucco, Tom. "Hunt for Haunts." http://www.sptimes.com/2002/10/31/TampaBay/Hunt_for_haunts.shtml.

Interviews

Coleman, Eddie. Personal interview. September 18, 2012.

Culpepper, Marilyn. Personal interview. November 1, 2003.

Dobosz, Pat. Personal interview. September 21, 2013

Gatti, Tom. Personal Interview. June 13, 2014.

Lewis, Trent. Personal interview. September 12, 2012.

Mahoney, Eileen. Personal interview. March 13, 2012.

Moode, Steve. Personal interview. July 12, 2002.

Obertson, Bonnie. Personal interview. July 9, 2010.

Redman, Joel. Personal interview. September 3, 2012.

Smollen, Shirley. Personal interview. July 18, 2009

Sutton, Sharon. Personal interview. July 30, 2012.

Newspapers

Livingston, Brian. "Ghost Hunters Visit Old Lauderdale County Jail." *Meridian (MS) Star*, October 29, 2012.

Robinson, Bill. "Ghost Hunters Detect Spirits at Boone Tavern." *Richmond Register*, April 2, 2012. http://www.richmondregister.com/localnews/x145100306`/Ghost-hunters-detect-spirits-at...

Warner, Penny. "The Galloway Ghost—1998." *Arkansas Democrate-Gazette*, October 1998. http://www.argenweb.net/white/wchs/The_Galloway_Ghost_files/The_Galloway_Ghost_1...

Video

Finn, Lillian. *The Owners of Goodwood Plantation*. Margaret E. Wilson Foundation and Goodwood Museum and Gardens.

ABOUT THE AUTHOR

Dr. Alan Brown is a professor of English at the University of West Alabama. Alan has written over a dozen books on ghosts and hauntings. He is an avid history buff and deeply involved in paranormal research and investigation. He is also affiliated with the American Folklore Society, the American Ghost Society and the Central Mississippi Paranormal Society.